Who Was
Armistead Burt?

1802 ❧❦ 1883

very sincerely yours,

Armistead Burt.

Armistead Burt
The Center Of
The Southern
Leadership Network

1802 ❧ 1883

by S. Robert Lathan, Jr. M.D.

very sincerely yours.

Armistead Burt.

WINGS
PUBLISHERS

Published by
Ginger Watkins
Wings Publishers, LLC
P O Box 2536
Boca Grande, Fl 33921

Text @ 2017 by S. Robert Lathan, Jr,

Design and Layout by Nicola Simmonds Carmack

Manufactured in the United States of America.

10987654321
First Edition

ISBN
978-1-930897-24-3

To the Archivists and Librarians

who by definition

*collect and select for permanent
or long term preservation of materials
on grounds of their enduring, cultural,
or evidentiary value*

Acknowledgements

To these institutions and individuals who enthusiastically provided to me reams of information to understand Armistead Burt.

Amy McDonald, Archivist
David M. Rubenstein, Rare Book & Manuscript Library
Duke University, Durham, NC

Henry G. Fulmer, Director & Mike Berry, Head of User Services
South Caroliniana Library
University of South Carolina, Columbia, SC

Jim Cross, Manuscript Archivist
Special Collections Unit
Clemson University Library, Clemson, SC

Robert M. Burts, Jr. "The Life of Armistead Burt"
Thesis submitted for Masters of Arts, 1945,
Duke University, Durham, NC

Bobby Edmonds, Historian and Author
McCormick, SC

May Hutchinson, descendant of Townes Robertson
509 N. Main Street, Abbeville, SC

Jane Nardy, Historian and Genealogist
Cashiers Historical Society, Cashiers, NC

John Barrow, Researcher
McKee Properties, Cashiers, NC

Ginger Watkins, Editor and Publisher
Boca Grande, FL

Millie Lathan, my wife
An extraordinary Partner on all my endeavors

To the Reader

This book began with a "Ramble" to Abbeville, South Carolina, led by Jane Nardy, Cashiers, NC premier historian and a noted genealogist. The purpose of the trip was to discover what could be learned about Armistead Burt, one of the early owners of the Cashiers Historical Society's National Register property, the Zachary-Tolbert House. Burt's story had been eclipsed by that of the Zacharys and the Tolberts and most knew nothing about this shadowy, brief summer resident of Cashiers, except his name. It appeared that he had left behind only his elegantly written signature as graffiti in the hallway of the house.

The "Ramble" for me extended into a decade long quest to discover who was this Armistead Burt who had been in the elite circle of plantation owners of upper South Carolina, in whose house Jefferson Davis' last cabinet meeting of the Confederacy had been held, who was a close friend and personal attorney of Wade Hampton III, and who had also become a confidant and advisor to Thomas Clemson. At the very least, had he not been an articulate witness to one of the most turbulent times in American history, the Civil War and Reconstruction? Why did so few know his name and none ever bothered to find a photograph or a portrait?

Many have guided and joined me in the search of discovery. Keven Hawkins would share his knowledge about Robert Burts' 1945 Master's Thesis on Armistead Burt at Duke University Library. May Hutchinson would open her historic house where Burt had later boarded and tell her many family stories. Countless archivists and librarians would aid in research. From the Library of Congress, to Duke University, to Clemson University, and to the South Caroliniana Library, so many professionals returned my calls and continually searched for information about this man. The staff at the South Caroliniana Library under the direction of Henry Fulmer cannot be lauded enough for their time and effort in gathering so many hand written and thankfully typed documents. And it would be Bobby Edmonds, author and historian, who not only shared his own library containing Calhoun's letters, but introduced me to the important link of the nineteenth century educator, Moses Waddel.

And my special recognition goes to my editor and publisher, Ginger Watkins, who took all the research and tied it together with imagination and thoroughness. She is the one who got it done.

While any photograph of Burt is yet to surface, my hope is for the reader to realize that a ramble through history can still uncover a fascinating story in the life of one heretofore forgotten South Carolinian who was the network center of the people and events which were to become a major turning point in American history.

S. Robert Lathan, Jr. MD
Author and Collector
April 10, 2018

Introduction

What was he really like? We have no pictures, no portraits of Armistead Burt, no recordings of his voice, and must therefore rely on his letters and writings, as well as those from his friends and contemporaries.

And why was Burt important? Armistead Burt's life demonstrates his ability to represent his constituents to the US Congress with the strongest intellect and endure the Civil War and Reconstruction in the South by utilizing his legal talents to further the values of respect and fairness. His astute legal counsel to his friends as well as his success in the courtrooms was respected all over South Carolina.

Burt was a relative and also a disciple of John C. Calhoun. Along with close friend, George McDuffie, he supported the Doctrine of Nullification with zeal and ability. His personal legal counsel benefitted his very close friend, Wade Hampton III, as well as the estates of the Clemson family. While considered an iconic figure in the courtroom, he was also a caring friend in attending to Calhoun, McDuffie, and Clemson during times of their poor health and to Jefferson Davis and his family in their time of great stress.

Burt and his prominent friends corresponded and visited often. From South Carolina in the early 19 th century, these individual leaders combined deep intellectual thinking with political skills in support of their home state of South Carolina. They joined together in the United States capitol of Washington, DC and in the state capitol of Columbia, SC. Their homes and retreats in the Pendleton District, Fort Hill, (now Clemson) and in Abbeville, SC and Cashiers, NC as well as the Springs in Virginia were their gathering places. The communication network of Burt and these Southern leaders positively influenced their communities for many years.

Armistead Burt
John C. Calhoun
Thomas Green Clemson
Jefferson Davis
Wade Hampton III
George McDuffie
Moses Waddel

Southern Leadership Network

The Leaders

Thomas G. Clemson
1807 – 1888

Edgefield District, SC

Pendleton District, SC

Brussels, Belgium

Fort Hill Plantation, SC

Wade Hampton III
1818 – 1902

Wildwoods Plantation, SC

Columbia, SC

Cashiers, NC

Armistead Burt
1802 – 1883

Orange Hill Plantation,
Abbeville District, SC

Abbeville, SC

Cashiers, NC

John C. Calhoun
1782 – 1850

Bath Plantation,
Abbeville District, SC

Washington, DC

Fort Hill Plantation,
Pendleton District, SC

George McDuffie
1790 – 1851

Edgefield District, SC

Cherry Hill Plantation,
Abbeville District, SC

Moses Waddel
1770-1840

Willington Academy,
Abbeville District, SC

Athens, Georgia

Southern Leadership Network
The Relationships

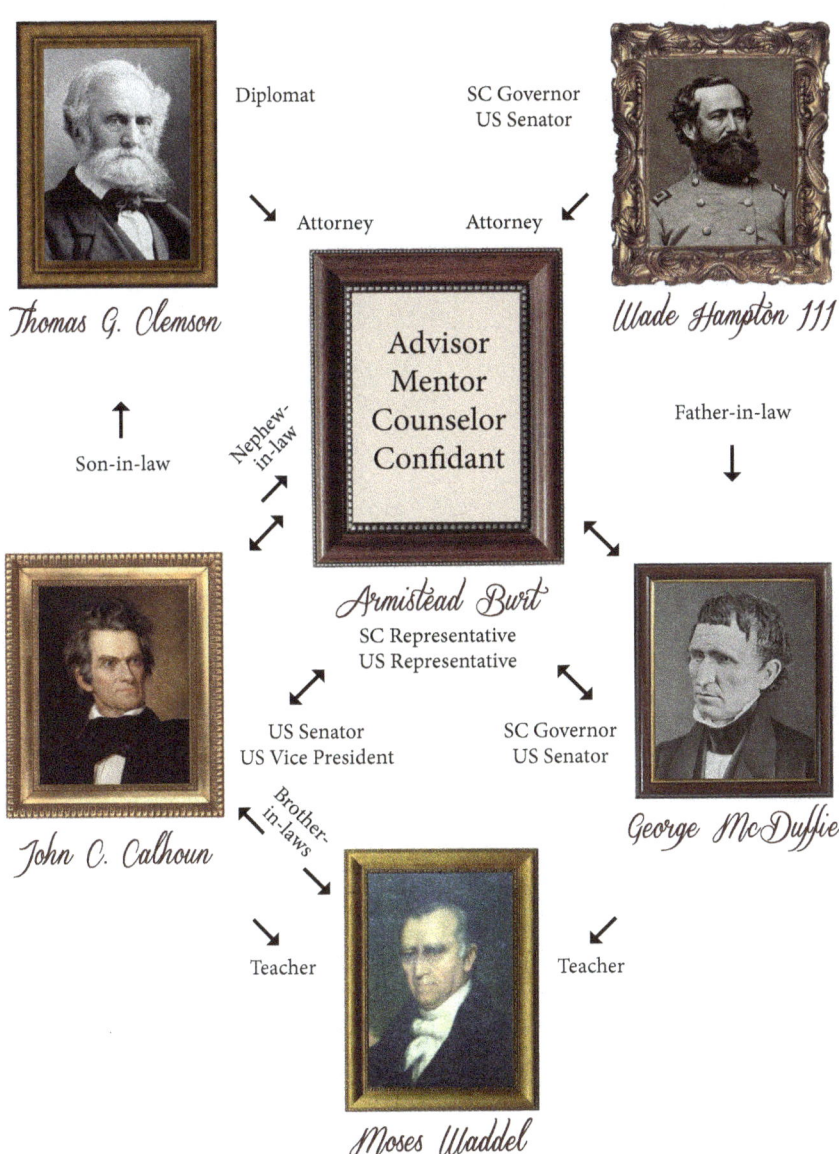

Thomas G. Clemson

Diplomat

Attorney

SC Governor
US Senator

Attorney

Wade Hampton III

Advisor
Mentor
Counselor
Confidant

Son-in-law

Nephew-in-law

Father-in-law

Armistead Burt
SC Representative
US Representative

John C. Calhoun

US Senator
US Vice President

SC Governor
US Senator

George McDuffie

Brother-in-laws

Teacher

Teacher

Moses Waddel

Southern Leadership Network
The Places, Abbeville District

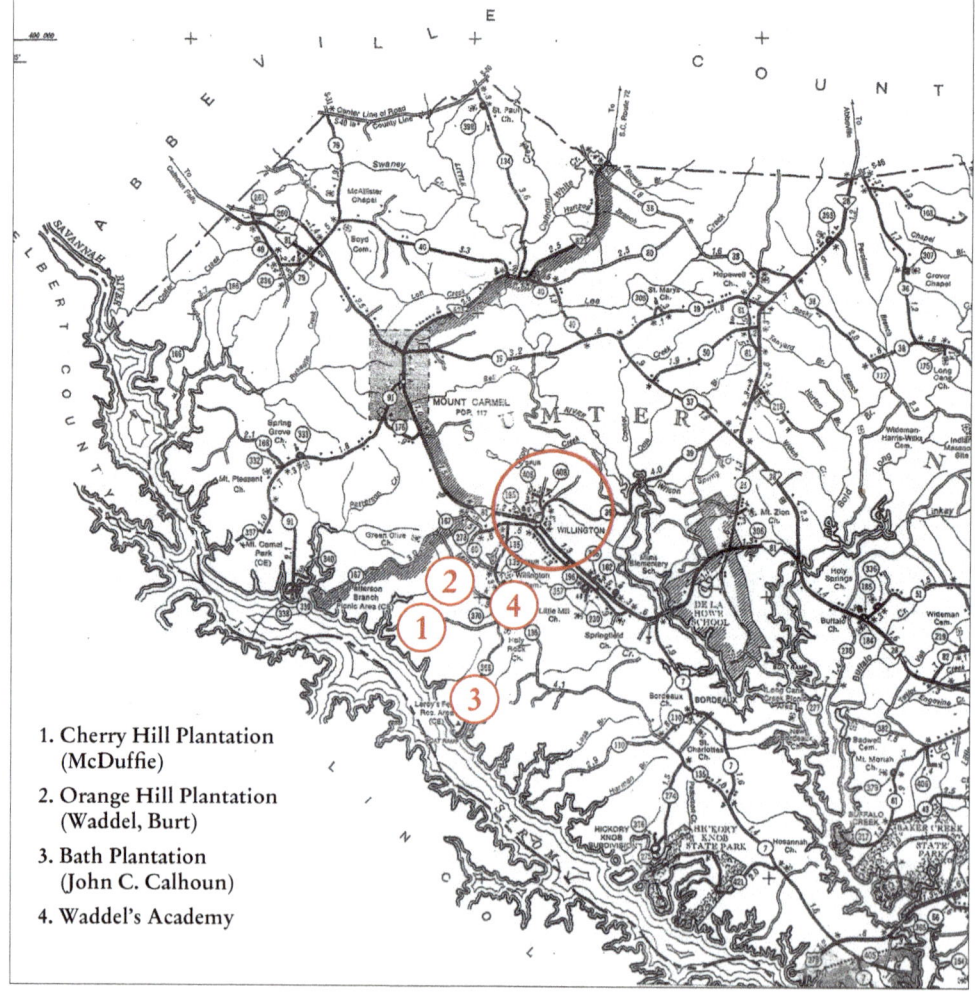

1. Cherry Hill Plantation (McDuffie)
2. Orange Hill Plantation (Waddel, Burt)
3. Bath Plantation (John C. Calhoun)
4. Waddel's Academy

Southern Leadership Network
The Places–Midlands & Upstate Regions

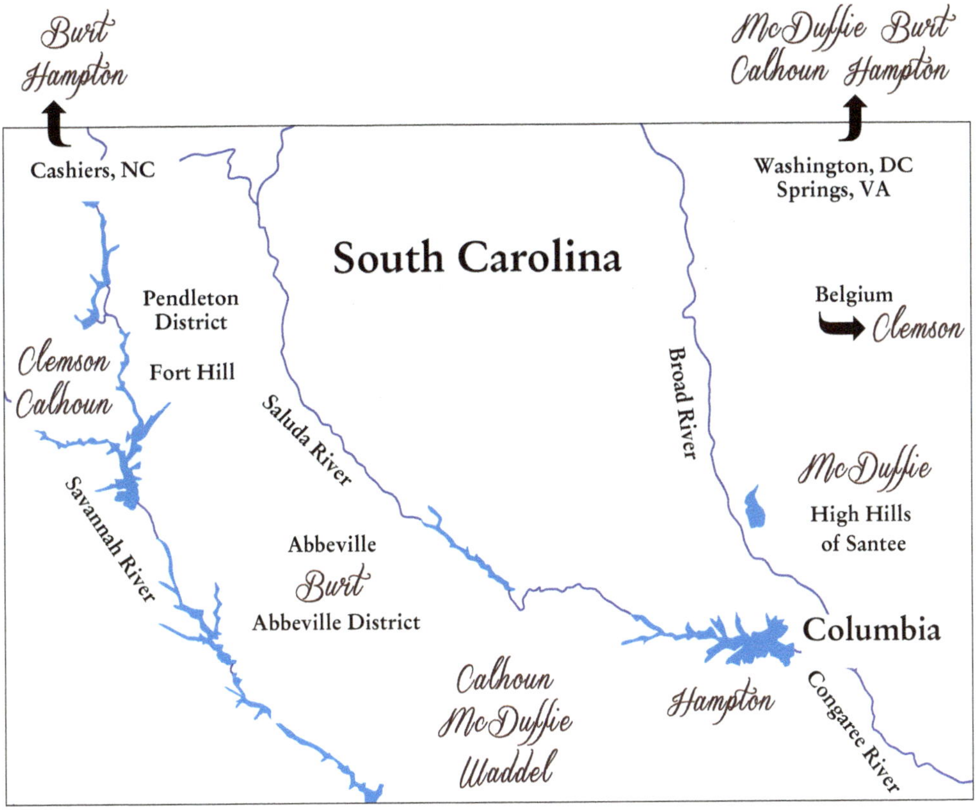

Burt
Hampton

McDuffie Burt
Calhoun Hampton

Cashiers, NC

Washington, DC
Springs, VA

South Carolina

Pendleton
District

Belgium
Clemson

Clemson
Calhoun

Fort Hill

Saluda River

Broad River

McDuffie

High Hills
of Santee

Savannah River

Abbeville

Burt

Abbeville District

Calhoun
McDuffie
Waddel

Hampton

Columbia

Congaree River

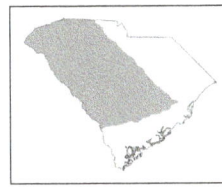

SOUTH CAROLINA

BURT-STARK HOUSE

When Jefferson Davis, President of the Confederacy, left Richmond after its fall in April 1865, he traveled south, trying to reach and rally the remnants of his army. On May 2, he spent the night at the home of Col. Armistead Burt. In 1971, Burt's great-niece Mary Stark Davis gave this historic house and all its furnishings to Abbeville's Historic Preservation Commission.

South Carolina honors Armistead Burt

Armistead Burt

The Center Of
The Southern Leadership Network

1802 ❧❧ 1883

The Burt family immigrated to Virginia from France. Matthew and Ann Burt moved in 1792, to the Edgefield District in South Carolina. Their son Francis was the oldest of eighteen children. Born in Virginia in 1759, Francis served as a soldier in the Continental Army during the Revolutionary War. In 1794, he married Katherine Miles, a descendant of French Huguenots, who lived with her family in the Beaufort District of South Carolina.

Born on November 13, 1802, at the Burt homestead on Cloud's Creek, Edgefield, SC, Armistead Burt was one of the five sons of Francis and Katherine of which two were lawyers, and three doctors. The three doctors all moved to Alabama in the 1830s to practice medicine. In 1807, Francis Burt moved his family to the Pendleton District in upstate South Carolina. This prosperous agricultural area was an active trading center located at the foot of the Blue Ridge Mountains. Armistead was taught by Mary Hunter, a local teacher, until deemed sufficiently trained to attend the Pendleton Male Academy with studies including Latin, Greek and oratory. Burt did not attend college and instead prepared for entrance in the field of law. He began the practice of law in the office of Warren R. Davis and was admitted to the Bar in 1823, at the age of 21.

In 1828, Burt married Martha Catherine Calhoun of Abbeville, the daughter of Catherine de Graffenried Calhoun and William "Cotton Billy" Calhoun (brother of John C.

Calhoun.) Having been in the Abbeville District for many years, the area was referred to as a community of Calhoun Settlements. "Cotton Billy" earned his nickname due to the fortune he accumulated in cotton. The young couple moved to the town of Abbeville, county seat of the Abbeville District, where Burt continued his law practice and Martha became a leader in all of the social circles.

Burt first knew his wife's famous uncle John Calhoun as a Pendleton neighbor and as a frequent guest at Burt's home in Abbeville. Their frequent communications with each other were both personal and political. Burt's involvement in politics came naturally and began soon upon moving to Abbeville with Calhoun becoming his confidant and mentor.

The gradual growth of opposition to the federal tariff of 1824, increased with the passage of the Tariff of Abominations in 1828. As Vice President of the United States, John Calhoun was working to modify the tariff and wrote to Burt in 1831 that he felt the burden of the taxes would be "taken off the North and left on the South; off the rich and left on the poor."[1]

Burt supported Calhoun's opposition to the tariff and spoke at public dinners honoring Calhoun at Pendleton. With the growing concerns over the economic future of the South their correspondence related mainly to political matters. Burt was truly a disciple of his uncle-in-law, John C. Calhoun and supported the doctrine of nullification with zeal, speaking at gatherings of the "Nullifiers" and meetings on "States' Rights." Those opposed, he called "union men."

Burt was elected as one of the six Abbeville delegates to the called state convention in November of 1832, and was appointed secretary of the convention. George McDuffie was another of the Abbeville delegates to the convention. After much debate, the Ordinance of Nullification declaring the federal tariff on South Carolina null and void, passed the convention by a large majority. All six of the delegates from Abbeville voted for nullification. McDuffie was chosen to deliver the "Address to the People of the United States" about the Ordinance of Nullification.

After resigning as Andrew Jackson's Vice President and becoming US Senator from South Carolina, Calhoun followed closely the events in South Carolina while in Congress and early in 1833, along with Henry Clay, called for a compromise on the tariff creating a gradual reduction of duties. Calhoun wrote to Burt, "If the tariff be not adjusted, the South will be busted in six months."[2]

In 1834, Burt was elected to the state legislature, along with four other Abbeville residents, serving for three sessions 1834-1835, 1838-1839, and 1840-1841. Burt participated in many committees and was chairman of several. He presented petitions, bills, reports, and resolutions. Most of the petitions in his time were of the local nature demonstrating his interest in the Abbeville constituents. His manners were considered stiff and precise, while his conversations and writings showed wit and humor. "He was highly popular by his fellow members."[3] The state legislature at this time was dominated by supporters of "states' rights" and strongly under the influence of US Senator John C. Calhoun.

Armistead Burt campaigned in 1842, for the U.S. House of Representatives in the fifth congressional district, which included Abbeville, Lexington, Edgefield, and Newberry counties. Members of Congress were among the very few elected officials chosen by the people instead of by the state legislature, requiring that candidates had to rigorously campaign within their districts. In one of Burt's speeches from the courthouse at Edgefield he said that he was born "only a stone's throw from that very spot." An editorial in the *Edgefield Advertizer* noted that Burt "had brilliant talents, high character, and extensive information upon the great subjects agitating the country."[4] In speeches in rural areas of his district, Burt emphasized that he was a planter and had been raised on a farm. In the election of 1842, he won a majority of votes over his two opponents.

In December 1843, Burt was present on the opening of the Twenty-Eighth Congress. He served in the House while Calhoun and McDuffie served in the Senate. "We doubt that the state has ever been better represented in Congress than at the present time. With John C. Calhoun and George McDuffie in the Senate and Rhett, Woodward, Burt, Simms, Black, and Holmes in the House, we venture the assertion that no state can present a greater array of talent and excellence."[5]

Burt sat in Congress for ten years, serving on the Judiciary Committee and acting as chair of the Military Affairs Committee. He also briefly served as Speaker Pro Tempore during the absence of Speaker Winthrop in 1848. Demonstrating his knowledge of parliamentary procedure, Burt took an active part in congressional debates and discussions disciplining himself to follow a personal set of rules that included "speak seldom, speak slowly,....and peruse the speeches of Hayne and Calhoun."[6]

A focus of Burt's attention while serving on Congressional committees was the expansion of the US through either treaty or war. Once the territorial boundaries were set, problems always faced the Military Affairs Committee as to the disposition of the soldiers and payment of volunteers. Burt consistently opposed the reduction of the Army and defended the increases in the appropriations bills "to protect the new lands that have come into our possession."[7] Much of the national debate in the sessions of 1849 and 1850 were concentrated on what Congress should do with respect to slavery in the western territories. Burt took little part in these debates. He did sign the "Southern Address," a paper drawn by John C. Calhoun. Burt was an accepted spokesman in the House for Calhoun's pro-southern policy, particularly states' rights, the reduction of tariffs, and maintaining the balance between slave and free states as the country expanded into the western territories.

As a member of Congress during the time of growing opposition to slavery in the western territories, Burt was in close touch with events preceding the secessionist movement of the South, especially in South Carolina. In a letter to the *Edgefield Advertizer* Burt set forth his ideas on the impending movement. He felt that "secession was not feasible and would involve the state in hostile collision with the national government and defeat would be the result of the unequal struggle." [8] Burt was clear about his moderate views.

"Martha Burt did not always accompany her husband to Washington. Most of the time, she remained in South Carolina to manage, with the help of a superintendent, the plantation named Orange Hill. Burt wrote her daily and described in minute detail the happenings in the capital."[9]

On those occasions when Martha Burt joined him in Washington, they stayed in highest style in a private apartment. Martha was fond of social life and together they attended balls and receptions.

While in Washington alone, Burt lived a rather secluded life and spent much time alone in study. He lived at a Washington boarding house and for a time stayed at the same hotel as Calhoun. On one occasion, Burt wrote that it cost him $10 per week to live in Washington. He was close to Calhoun and McDuffie and his letters mention his concern about their ailing health. During Calhoun's final illness in March 1850, Burt was with him two or three times a day, making arrangements for his care.[10]

There was evidence in Burt's political career that he was not completely happy with his life in Washington. He on one occasion described himself as "the lonely tenant of the prison performing the task of counting minutes as they drag heavily along."[11] His health was very poor during the last session in Congress and in 1852, the following announcement appeared in the a district newspaper…"the announcement of his determination not to be a candidate again and return to South Carolina to remain in retirement."[12]

In March 1853, Burt made the public statement, "I am passionately fond of the pursuits of a planter and shall devote much time to agriculture."[13]

Burt retired from Congress to Orange Hill, a beautiful home and thriving plantation in the lower part of Abbeville County near the Savannah River. Orange Hill adjoined Cherry Hill, George McDuffie's former home and plantation. Before McDuffie died in 1851, he had been a close friend and political associate of Burt.

Burt's farming operations were extensive requiring the management of a superintendent and a multitude of workers. Cotton was the chief money producing crop with also the addition of potatoes, peas, grains, grapes and fruit orchards.

Besides devoting time to the agricultural success of the plantation, Burt also participated in local politics, voicing a moderate approach to secession. He was active in the Abbeville Democratic Club and chairman of the Abbeville Committee of the Kansas Association, which sought to enlist emigrants to Kansas to ensure a pro-slavery population in the new territories and states. Burt spoke at public gatherings to urge enlistments and financial support for those people who would move to Kansas.[14] In 1856, he urged the renomination of Franklin Pierce for his second term of President of the United States. Pierce lost the nomination to James Buchanan.

In 1858, he moved from his plantation to Abbeville to focus on his law practice. His and Martha's new residence was purchased from Andrew Simond and was one of the most beautiful homes in Abbeville with white columns, magnolia trees, hedges, shrubbery and numerous fountains. A visitor remarked that the Burt home combines to rare degree…"comfort and elegance hardly found elsewhere."[15]

On November 18, 1860, the Burts were baptized at the Trinity Episcopal Church in Abbeville. A few months later in 1861, the Burts donated the "Bishops Chair" to the church and participated actively in church activities.

After Abraham Lincoln was elected President of the United State in 1860, the South Carolina legislature issued a call for a convention to consider the relation to the Union. Abbeville was one of the first districts to respond to the call. A mass meeting was convened on the north side of an amphitheatrical hill (now called Secession Hill) to support severance from the Union. Burt did not speak at this mass meeting indicating that his feelings on the severity of secession had not changed. David Lewis Wardlaw a conservative friend of Burt's did speak and was "booed."[16]

In December 1860, the South Carolina state convention in Charleston passed the Ordinance of Secession by a unanimous vote with Burt present.

One month later on January 2, 1861, Burt was elected Commissioner to the State of Mississippi and attended their convention in Jackson to convince the state of Mississippi to join South Carolina. From the beginning of the talks of secession, Burt had urged South Carolina to act only in

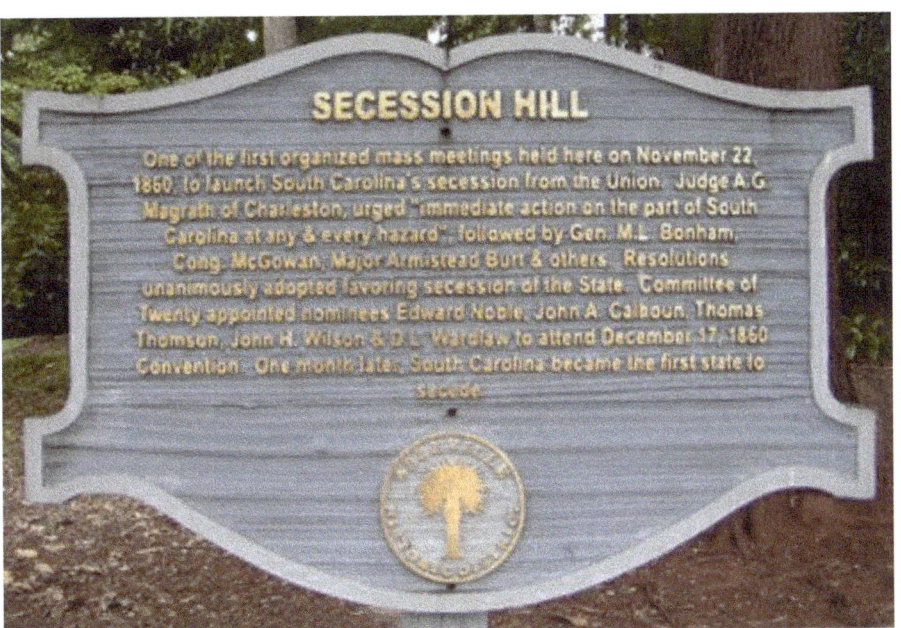

*The hill was known as Magazine Hill for a
"powder magazine" located there.
Armistead Burt was present at the meeting, but did not speak.*

cooperation with other southern states. He wrote to South Carolina Governor Pickens that the "people of Mississippi are thoroughly aroused and animated by the noblest sentiments."[17]

Burt was too old for active military service and became a soldier on the home front supervising enlistments and presiding at local meetings. He offered his service to the Confederacy and was replied to by his close friend Jefferson Davis. "I am in receipt of your letter.... you furnish another evidence of the patriotic zeal which prompts men of the highest position to labor wherever needed.."[18]

One of the wartime activities performed by Burt was to be custodian of the property of the local soldiers. "If you can spare the time, a visit once a week to my farm would, I know, keep my affairs in trim," wrote one soldier.[19]

By the spring of 1865, the Confederacy had suffered large losses and the war was drawing to an end. General Lee, threatened with envelopment, decided to concentrate his troops on the southwest of Richmond, notifying the government officials to leave the city. Varina Howell Davis, First Lady of the Confederate States and her children were part of the evacuation force.

In April 1865, Mrs. Davis and her family stayed in the Burt house for twelve days after they fled Richmond to avoid capture by the Union troops. Initially she refused to stay in the home fearing it might be destroyed for sheltering her and that she would be captured by the Federals. To this Burt replied, "I know of no better use to which my house could be put than to have it burned giving shelter to a friend."[20]

They left Abbeville two days before President Jefferson Davis, Secretary of War John C. Breckinridge, and the Confederacy's senior military advisors arrived in Abbeville. Burt graciously opened his home to President Davis and the

Cabinet of the Confederacy for their Council meeting.

Burt's beautiful home had been a very popular social center in Abbeville. From 1858 to 1865, the Burt's lived in comfort and ease at their home and entertained extensively with nine servants. The Civil War brought an end to their extravagant lifestyle as the entire South was devastated. When Burt purchased his home, he did not pay for it in full. During the war, with a decreased income, he made some payments with Confederate money. In 1868, his creditor A. J. Simond insisted on a settlement of Burt's debt and also to give further lien on his plantation, Orange Hill. The creditor then said that the "home and furnishings had cost him about $10,000 in gold, and that the payments to Burt's indebtedness had been in Confederate money which was worth only five cents on the dollar."[21]

The loss of resources faced families whose wealth had stretched over several generations and several states such as the Wade Hampton III family who were forced to declare bankruptcy on some of their properties. Through this trying time, spirits were bolstered by the shared friendships and troubles. In 1868, Burt received a letter from Mary Hampton, Wade Hampton's wife, requesting a loan of $100 until the return of Hampton from his properties in Mississippi.

After the war, the health of Martha Burt began failing, and she died on March 27, 1869, about one month after the Burts left their large home and moved to the Marshall House, the village hotel. Martha was remembered in the local press for her "brilliancy and culture and many friends…"[22] Later Burt lived at the home of a friend, J. Townes Robertson. Burt became as one of the family at the Robertson's home.

Even with the devastation of the economy, and the loss of family members, homes and land holdings all over the South, the leaders like Burt were still active in attempting to keep their communities together trying to create futures for their families though in unknown directions. A first sign of new action came in June 1865, immediately after the war, when President Andrew Johnson appointed Benjamin Perry, an Abbevillian, as the provisional governor.

Perry was tasked with the responsibility of calling a constitutional convention to declare slavery abolished and provide for the elections of US Senators and Congressmen. The convention met in September 1865, and amongst its actions, created a commission to develop a code for the regulation of labor.

Perry appointed Burt and David Wardlaw as the two commissioners to draft the "Black Codes" to regulate the movement of former slaves. Burt's appointment was thought to be "worthily bestowed."[23] Burt and Wardlaw had previously made news together in the famous Yancey trial in Greenville, SC in 1838. While charged with the task of creating laws that would move the newly freed slaves, the Federal government found the codes lacking and forced the state legislature to modify them. In 1867, South Carolina became part of the Second Military District under the Congressional Reconstruction Act.

Burt continued his Abbeville law practice while participating in the movement to remove the state's radical Republican leadership in the State Convention of 1868. Burt served as president of the first Convention of South Carolina Democratic Clubs as well as a delegate to the National Democratic convention in New York. In 1868, the Republicans carried the November election. The Democrats carried only a few counties including Abbeville, Anderson and Newberry in which Burt had spoken previously. Burt participated in the Taxpayer's Convention in 1871 and 1874, preparing reports detailing corruption within state government. All contributed to the fight against the radicals.

Robert K. Scott of Ohio was the first Republican governor in South Carolina. His administration, from 1868 to 1872, was guilty of almost every description of corruption. The legislature at the time was composed of temporary visitors from the Union called "carpetbaggers" and newly freed slaves. Scott was accused of bribery and extravagant expenditures. By 1870, the state debt had reached $7,665,908.98.[24]

During the Second Taxpayers Convention in 1874, Burt was chosen chairman of a committee charged with preparing a written presentation to Congress to review the evils of all the branches of the South Carolina state government. Burt urged that it was to the interest of both races to unite to secure relief from the oppressive taxation and "other evils which have come upon the state."[25] When presenting the paper reviewing the facts of the corruption, Burt found very little interest by President Grant or Secretary Fish.

Attempts at reform met with little success prior to 1874, when opposition among the more conservative Republicans elected Daniel H. Chamberlain of Massachusetts as governor in 1874. In many ways, Chamberlain's administration was one of reform and corrected the abuses of the radical Republican regime until the election of two disreputable characters to the circuit court bench. It had taken until 1872, for the US Congress to pass the Amnesty Act, restoring the voting rights to soldiers and officers who participated in the Civil War, thus increasing the voting base of Democrats in South Carolina.

In 1875, shortly after the election of the very unpopular circuit court judges, Martin Witherspoon Gary of Edgefield became the architect of a plan to excise the state from the Republican radicals by strengthening the Democratic Party. In 1876, Wade Hampton was nominated by the Democratic party for the governorship of South Carolina. Hampton

15

seemed to be the perfect candidate with his long and storied family history and his bravery in the Civil War. The fact that Hampton had been out of the state much of the time since the war had kept him removed from many controversies. As Wade Hampton's lawyer, mentor, and intimate political confidant, Burt and Hampton spent much time together in South Carolina and in Cashiers, North Carolina. Wade Hampton wrote in 1868, that there was "no one and whose judgments. . .I would fully confide than yourself, and you are the only one I can consult."[26]

Burt supported Hampton full heartedly in the 1876 campaign. When Hampton visited Abbeville, Burt welcomed him at the depot and had Hampton as his guest that night in the Norwood home.

In the election, both sides claimed victory. On April 11, 1877, after President Hayes withdrew Federal troops, the Republican officers agreed with Chamberlain that further resistance was futile and turned the executive offices over to Hampton. Burt was instrumental in Hampton's election as South Carolina's first post-Reconstruction governor and wrote, "This is the first time in nine years that South Carolinians had the privilege of paying taxes to a government of their own choice."[27] Governor Hampton soon severed his relationship with Gary due to Gary's controversial election tactics.

Burt's longest uninterrupted work in law practice came after the Civil War and during the decade of 1870 to 1880. His practice included both criminal and civil cases, with a predominance of the latter as revealed in his letters. He was described as being "a power in the Appellate Courts and always being heard with close attention."[28] His income from law was small during the last years of his life and was indicated by the condition of his estate at his death, "appraised at only $275.00."[29]

The volume of his practice, his success at winning cases, and praise of his work by his contemporaries indicated that he was a lawyer of more than ordinary ability. His work record in the Court of Appeals shows him appearing twenty-seven times in ten years. His cases in general varied from support of bank charters, defending accused murderers and even winning a case in support of a Negro woman for carrying a concealed weapon because she was a "Woman" and existing law was only for "Men."

At his death in 1883, one of Burt's contemporaries said, "(As a lawyer) he was a hard worker; he was painstaking; he had an acute intellect and a sleepless vigilance; his skill in handling cases before juries was superior; he was sympathetic with the young lawyers at the bar; his client was his first concern; his deportment was courteous, fluid and firm."[30]

The veteran Clerk of Court for Abbeville County remembered Burt as being "tall, handsome, well-dressed and rather cold and stiff in his manners." A letter later said he was "an aristocrat and did not care for commonality and was sarcastic in his examination of witnesses."[31]

Previously in 1873, Burt had purchased a home and small farm in Cashiers Valley, Jackson County, North Carolina. Mordecai Zachary, a skilled carpenter had built the Greek revival-styled boarding house in the 1850s, and had built the hunting lodge for Wade Hampton in 1856, also in Cashiers. Burt called his new purchase his "mountain house," spending many months there every summer along with Thomas Clemson. Burt had also enjoyed going to the "Springs" in Virginia for his health along with Clemson, McDuffie, and Hampton.

In his declining years, Burt became a member of the Abbeville Literary Society and in 1877, presented to the society an essay on the "History of Abbeville" and also presented a paper on George McDuffie that contained a description of a duel in which McDuffie was a principal and Burt a second.

In 1881, Burt sold his mountain retreat in Cashiers, NC to William Henry Parker, the former mayor of Abbeville, SC. The records show that he paid Mordecai Zachary $700 for the home in 1873, and received $1,100 from Parker at the sale.

Burt was very lonely in his later years. He and Martha had been childless, and had no other near relatives. He often expressed that his death be sudden, without a long lingering illness.

"On October 30, 1883, Burt went to his law office. At noon, a servant from the Robertson home brought him lunch. He complained of not feeling well and sent for a glass of milk. It was his custom to lie down on a couch in his office after lunch. Later in the evening a boy, from the local newspaper called to carry a proof for Burt to read. The boy found Burt dead on the couch. About him were the law books he loved so well."[32] The body was carried to the home of Townes Robertson where Burt had been living. The next day Burt was buried in the cemetery at Trinity Episcopal Church in Abbeville next to his wife Martha Calhoun Burt.

Martha and Armistead Burt's headstone in Trinity Episcopal Church

Locations of Burt Homes

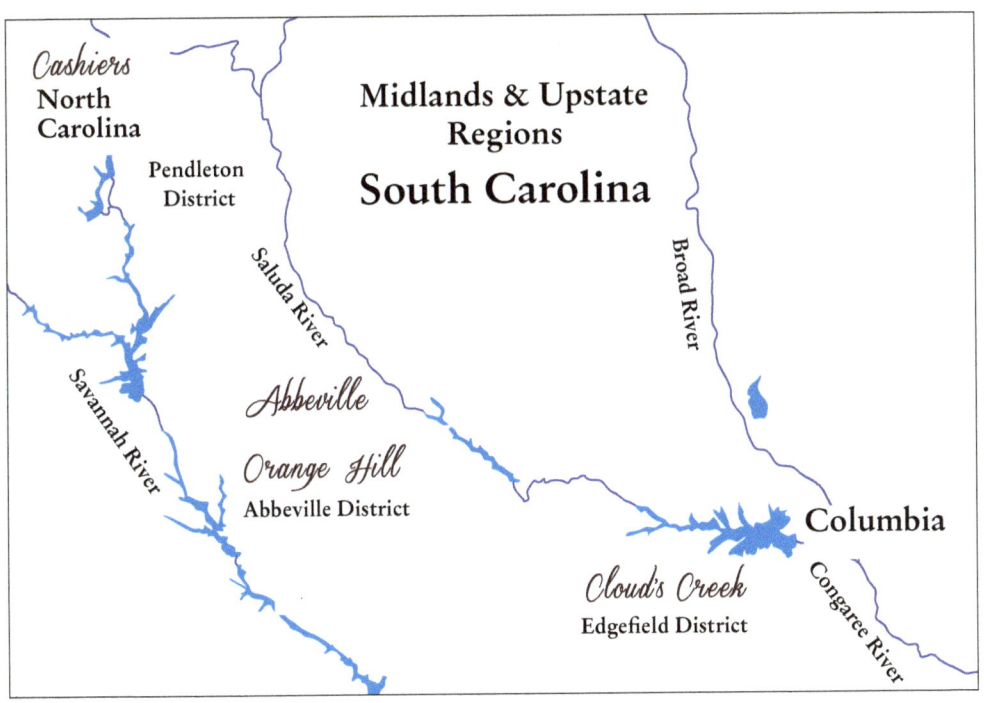

Homes of Burt from birth in 1802
to death in 1883

The Homes Of Armistead Burt

1802
Born at the Burt family homestead on Cloud's Creek, Edgefield District, SC

1807
Moved with family to farm in Pendleton District, SC

1828
Married Martha Calhoun and moved to town of Abbeville

1830s
Purchased the Orange Hill Plantation in Abbeville County on the Savannah River

1858
Purchased a Greek Revival house in Abbeville, later called the Burt Stark Mansion and made a National Historic Landmark

1869
Sold the Burt Mansion and moved to Marshall Hotel

1870–1883
Lived in home of the James Townes Robertson family, 509 North Main Street, Abbeville, SC

1873–1881
Purchased a house in Cashiers, NC from Mordecai Zachery as a summer retreat. Sold house to William H. Parker

1883
Armistead Burt was buried in Trinity Cemetery

Orange Hill Plantation
Savannah River, Abbeville District

As Burt officially ended his career in the US Congress in 1853, he made a public statement as to his plans:

"I am passionately fond of the pursuits of a planter and shall devote much time to agriculture."[33]

After Congress, Burt and Martha spent most of their time at Orange Hill Plantation located in the lower part of Abbeville County. The name of the plantation came from the Osage orange trees that surrounded the house and well. The plantation had been purchased from the family of Reverend Moses Waddel. Reverend Waddel had founded the famous Willington Academy in the same area. The educator had moved to Athens, GA to expand the University of Georgia.

The home had earlier burned and been rebuilt as a beautiful mansion with rows of stately crepe myrtles leading to the house from the roadway. The interior walls were lined with walnut that complimented the beautiful cypress wood exterior on top of a brick basement.

The farming operations were extensive with cotton as the primary money crop on over 2000 acres of land. Burt employed a superintendent with a large labor force to make the property profitable. Records indicate that other crops included vegetables, grains and even grapes and fruit trees.

Orange Hill Plantation was situated on the Savannah River next to the home of George McDuffie called Cherry Hill Plantation.

Burt and his wife chose to move to Abbeville in 1858 with the indication that this was not a financial decision, but a desire to again practice law. During Burt's financial problems after the Civil War, the records indicated that repayment of loans made on Orange Hill continued to add debts on to the Abbeville home as well as the Burts' social life style.

Orange Hill was sold to the Gilbert Family who added more acres and rebuilt the house. The property was then sold to Duke Power and later to the Army Corp of Engineers.

Armistead Burt House

Also known as
Burt-Stark Mansion
Abbeville, SC

The house is considered to be the architectural jewel of Abbeville, SC and was declared a National Historic Landmark in 1992.

David Lesley, an Abbeville attorney, built the house in the 1830s. Lesley sent a master carpenter to view a house he had seen as a copy for his new home in Abbeville. The house is a Greek Revival two story house with a frame structure and lap siding supported by four square columns on a brick foundation. Spacious rooms and high ceilings flank the large central hall with double doors opening to create a large ball-room. The gardens were designed by an English landscaper named Johnson. The narrow entrance drive circles before the front steps where a dismount stone still stands.

The house was owned by Lesley until his death in 1855, and then sold to Thomas A. Hoyt, a Presbyterian pastor. When Hoyt was transferred to another church, Andrew Simonds a banker bought it and sold to Burt.

For the next several years, Armistead and Martha Burt lived lavishly in Abbeville entertaining and sharing their home with friends and guests to the community. The elaborate and beautiful grounds had magnolia hedges and numerous fountains. A visitor remarked that the "Burt Home" combines

"comfort and elegance hardly found elsewhere. There is something very pleasing in the broad walks, in the scent of sweet shrubs, and in the well-trimmed hedges."[34]

Burt sold the house to a local planter, James Norwood in 1869. James Samuel Stark purchased the house in 1900. With his wife Stark restored the building and its furnishings. Later his family continued the restoration and preservation activities. On the death of his daughter in 1987, the house was given to the Abbeville Historic Commission. The house is now open to public tours by the Historic Commission.

Burt Stark House, center of social and political Abbeville

James Townes Robertson Home

In 1870, after the death of his wife Martha, Armistead Burt moved from the Marshall Hotel in Abbeville down the street to the home of James Townes Robertson. Only a few blocks from the Abbeville Court House, Burt had easy access to his law office and the necessary court appearances. While living in the Robertson's home, Burt was treated as family and enjoyed a formal dinner each night in the dining room.

Entrance to Robertson home on North Main Street

Robertson Family Tree

James Townes Robertson *married* Eugenia Anna Miller
1832–1905   1852–1894

↙ *Daughter*

Eugenia Miller Robertson *married* Charles Augustus Baskin, Sr.
1885–1962   1881–1931

↙ *Daughter*

May Robertson Baskin *married* Rufus Wood Hutchinson, Jr.
1922–   1917–2006

Robertson House dining room.
Mrs. May Hutchinson, 96 years old,
descendant and current owner

The Zachary Tolbert House
Cashiers, North Carolina

The Zachary Tolbert House was built in the Cashiers Valley of North Carolina by Mordecai Zachary beginning construction in 1842, and finishing almost ten years later. The house was built in the classic Greek Revival style that was popular at the time in the low country of South Carolina. The stately house and stable became a popular boarding house for travelers enjoying the cool summers and abundant hunting.

Mordecai Zachary was a son of Colonel John A. Zachary, one of the first settlers of the area. In the spring of 1833, Colonel Zachary (1779-1872), his wife Sarah and their thirteen children loaded wagons and migrated from Surry County, North Carolina traveling the trail to the Pickens area of South Carolina. From there they made their way northwest and, after weeks of traveling, finally arrived at their homestead. John Zachary chose the headwaters of the Chattooga River as the location for his new home. The Zacharys marked their claims of the land granted for homesteading to settlers by marking certain trees creating the boundary corners. It is said that the state of North Carolina, which disbursed and recorded the grants from the US government, received 5 cents per acre for these homestead grants.

Mordecai Zachary (1822-1896) spent his life in Cashiers Valley as a carpenter, saw and grist miller, innkeeper, and even the postmaster from 1855 to 1859. He and his wife Elvira Keener (1832-1913) had twelve children. Newly married M. Zachary and bride Elvira moved into the completed home in 1852. By census information, M. Zachary was one of the richest men in the area in land value and rental income from the properties.

In the 1850s, Wade Hampton III fell in love with the mountains surrounding the Cashiers Valley and stayed at Mordecai's stately rental boarding house. In 1855, Hampton paid Alexander Zachary, older brother of Modecai Zachary, $5 an acre for a 14 ½ acres portion of the original land grant in order to build a hunting cabin with rooms for many family members. After Hampton married Mary S. McDuffie, daughter of George McDuffie, in 1859, he brought his children and friends to spend their summers in Cashiers Valley.

In September 1873, Armistead Burt, from Abbeville, SC, bought the Greek Revival house, stable, and 75 acres from M. Zachary for $700. Burt paid $300 at the time and $400 a year later. The friendship of Wade Hampton was part of the desire to have a summer home in the area. Burt called his new purchase "his mountain house" and spent many summer months there along with Thomas Clemson and other South Carolinian friends.

In 1881, Burt sold the house and property to William Henry Parker (1828-1905) for $1100. Parker was also from Abbeville, SC and a former law partner of Burt and a member of the South Carolina House of Representatives. Parker was joined in the house by his brother, Francis Lejau Parker (1836-1913) from Charleston, SC. Francis Parker, a practicing physician and former Army doctor provided medical service to the community during his stay in Cashiers.

In 1901, the Parkers sold the house to Robert "Red" Tolbert (1863-1938) for $1650. Tolbert was a cotton farmer and prominent resident from Abbeville who continued the use of the house as a family summer retreat. The Tolbert family remained owners of the home until 1998, when the house was sold by Robert "Bubba" Tolbert, Jr., to Thomas C. and Wendy V. Dowden. The Dowdens sold the Zachary-Tolbert House and 4.21 acres to the Village Conservancy and then to the Cashiers Historical Society in July 2009. The house is posted on the National Register of Historic Places.

Last Council of War

Confederate States of America

Near the end of the Civil War, Jefferson Davis, the first and only President of the Confederate States of America became aware that Richmond would soon fall and prepared to send his family south. On March 29, 1865, Mrs. Davis and her four children left Richmond by train. On April 2, President Davis received a telegram from General Robert E. Lee that Richmond must be promptly evacuated. Davis then left by train for Danville, Virginia with his cabinet. At this point Davis had not thought of surrendering the Confederacy and did not consider his cause lost.

On Sunday, April 9, in a farmhouse in Appomattox Court House, VA, General Robert E. Lee surrendered the Army of Northern Virginia to General Ulysses S. Grant. Confederate General Joseph Johnston met with Union General William T. Sherman to negotiate the terms of the surrender, which included cessation of hostilities and safe passage for the Confederate soldiers to their homes as requested by President Abraham Lincoln. After Lincoln's assassination, Secretary of War Edward Stanton declared the agreement for safe passage null and void, requiring a second surrender by Johnston.

Davis and his advisors had immediately become fugitives forcing them to keep moving south hoping to reach the friendly troops in the Gulf States or even the Trans-Mississippi area for safety.

On May 2, 1865, the leaders of the Confederacy with President Davis reached the home of Armistead Burt in Abbeville, SC, a safe place to hold their Council of War meeting.

President Jefferson Davis presided at a cabinet meeting and on advice from his advisers, including General Braxton Bragg and four other brigade generals, Davis agreed that further resistance was impossible and that the Confederate cause was lost.

The cavalry officers said they were holding their men together only to prevent the capture of Davis and to help his escape. The "Council of War" discussed the possibility of safely reaching the Mississippi River. Traveling at the same time, but not in the same place, was an escorted wagon train carrying the Treasury of the Confederated States from Richmond, VA. A decision was made the next day to divide the Confederate Treasury partially to pay the escorting soldiers and to keep the rest of the wagons moving. The purported total amount to be $253,000.[35]

Davis appeared disappointed, and Burt tactfully led Davis to another room. Davis said, "We have lost. God knows that I did all in my power to save our beloved Confederacy."[34] About midnight, the presidential party prepared to continue the flight to Georgia.

Attendees

Jefferson Davis,
President

Judah B. Benjamin,
Secretary of State

John C. Breckenridge,
Secretary of War

S.R. Mallory,
Secretary of Navy

John R. Reagan,
Post Master

Brigade Generals

Braxton Bragg

S. W. Ferguson

George C. Dibrell

Basil Duke

Alfred Vaughan

W. C. Breckenridge

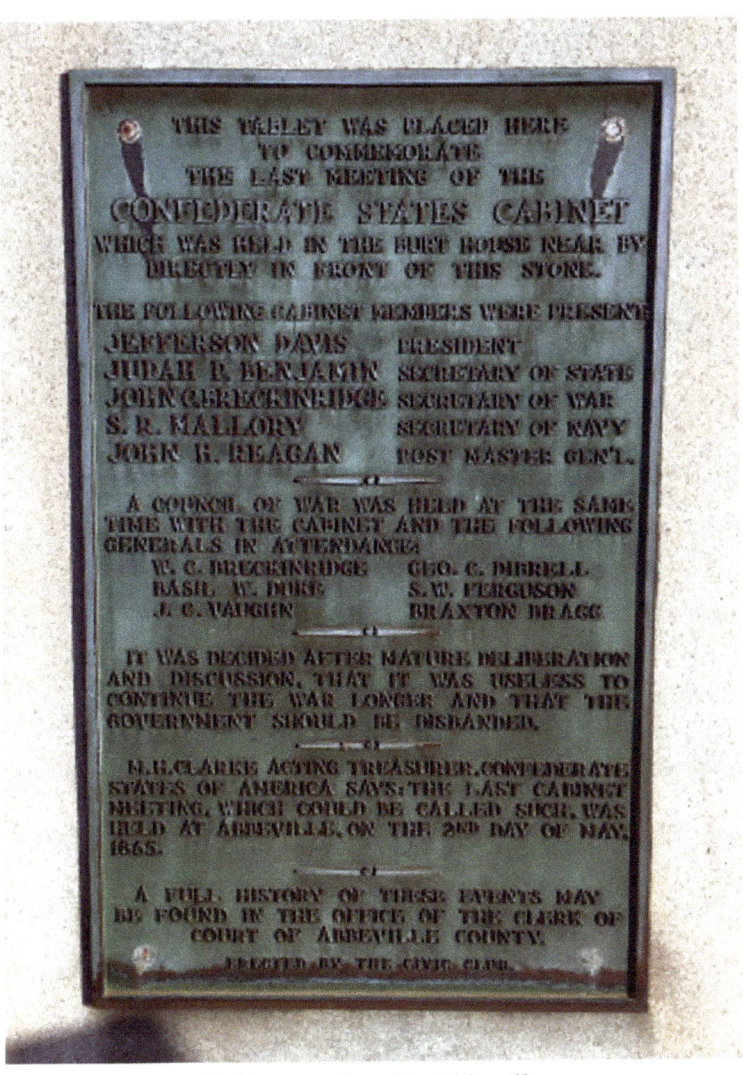

THIS TABLET WAS PLACED HERE
TO COMMEMORATE
THE LAST MEETING OF THE
CONFEDERATE STATES CABINET
WHICH WAS HELD IN THE BURT HOUSE NEAR BY
DIRECTLY IN FRONT OF THIS STONE.

THE FOLLOWING CABINET MEMBERS WERE PRESENT

JEFFERSON DAVIS — PRESIDENT
JUDAH P. BENJAMIN — SECRETARY OF STATE
JOHN C.BRECKINRIDGE — SECRETARY OF WAR
S. R. MALLORY — SECRETARY OF NAVY
JOHN H. REAGAN — POST MASTER GEN'L.

A COUNCIL OF WAR WAS HELD AT THE SAME
TIME WITH THE CABINET AND THE FOLLOWING
GENERALS IN ATTENDANCE:

W. C. BRECKINRIDGE   GEO. G. DIBRELL
BASIL W. DUKE   S.W. FERGUSON
J. C. VAUGHN   BRAXTON BRAGG

IT WAS DECIDED AFTER MATURE DELIBERATION
AND DISCUSSION, THAT IT WAS USELESS TO
CONTINUE THE WAR LONGER AND THAT THE
GOVERNMENT SHOULD BE DISBANDED.

M.H.CLARKE ACTING TREASURER, CONFEDERATE
STATES OF AMERICA SAYS; THE LAST CABINET
MEETING, WHICH COULD BE CALLED SUCH, WAS
HELD AT ABBEVILLE, ON THE 2ND DAY OF MAY,
1865.

A FULL HISTORY OF THESE EVENTS MAY
BE FOUND IN THE OFFICE OF THE CLERK OF
COURT OF ABBEVILLE COUNTY.

ERECTED BY THE CIVIC CLUB.

*Tablet was placed in Abbeville,
location of the Last Confederate Cabinet Meeting*

Last Council of War painting by Wilbur G. Kurtz given to city of Abbeville

The Missing Confederate Gold

The missing or lost Confederate gold has been a source of numerous legends especially in Georgia and perhaps also in South Carolina.

Several historians and writers have been uncertain as to the exact amount of the gold and silver carried south by the fleeing government. Numerous written articles have led to speculation and confusion. After I worked on this mystery, I concluded that one individual stood out.

He is Marshall (Mark) P. Waters III, PhD, of Washington, Georgia, who published outstanding reprints about ten years ago and has made many speeches on the subject. His articles are complete with a detailed bibliography showing evidence of his hard working research. His two main subjects are on the Confederate "treasury" and the "bank assets."

The government of the Confederacy abandoned its capital in Richmond, VA on Sunday, April 2, 1865, moving the treasury to Danville, VA. Stephen Russell Mallory, Confederate Secretary of the Navy, ordered Captain William Harwar Parker, CSN, the Superintendent of the Confederate Naval Academy, to command sixty midshipmen aged 14-18 of the Naval Academy to guard the Confederate treasury, which contained silver and gold coins later counted to be $327,022.90.

The assets of the six Richmond, VA banks were also counted and totaled $450,000 ($ 9 million today) of silver and gold coins. The bank assets were kept separate of the Confederate treasury, but moved together on the train from Richmond to Danville and then to Greensboro, NC.

On April 7, 1865, at Greensboro, NC $39,000 was paid out of the treasury to Gen. Joseph E. Johnston and his soldiers as well as $35,000 was taken for use of travel for President

Davis and the Cabinet. As the war ended, President Davis and his wife Varina retreated from Virginia to Washington, GA, near Irwinville, GA and at no time did Davis have the treasury funds in his possession.

On April 8, the treasury and the bank assets arrived in Charlotte, NC. The rail lines were open to Chester, SC but ended there so they were transferred to wagons on April 12 and then to Newberry, SC. They were then loaded again on rail lines and taken to Abbeville, SC on April 15. The next day wagons were loaded again with both treasury and bank assets to travel across the Savannah River by pontoon boat to Washington, GA.

On learning that General James H. Wilson, USA had captured Macon, GA, Capt Parker decided to move by train to Augusta, GA on April 18. Due to the pending fall of Augusta, Parker decided to turn the money over to the Davis entourage and returned back to Washington, GA by train on April 23 to load the treasury for travel back to Abbeville by wagons.

The bank assets of $450,000 were then deposited on April 24 to a Bank of Georgia branch in Washington, GA. On May 2, the Jefferson Davis party arrived in Abbeville. Then Navy Secretary Mallory ordered Parker to transfer the treasury to the Acting Secretary of the Treasury, John H. Reagan, who then instructed it be delivered to Brigadier General Basil W. Duke. Parker then disbanded the midshipmen as guards and sent them to their homes.

On May 2, President Davis held his Cabinet Meeting and Council of War meeting in Burt's home. Once finished Davis and the Generals attending, departed for different designations. Davis departed for Washington, GA hoping to reunite with his wife and family. About 4000 cavalry, the Confederate Secretary of War, General John C. Breckenridge, and the confederate treasury in wagons accompanied Davis.

On May 3, after crossing the Savannah River on the pontoon bridge, the party made camp about three miles inland. There a "mutiny" of sorts within the cavalry units occurred with the soldiers expressing their anxiety at having not been paid in months and that the chances of being seized by the Federal troops were very strong. Breckenridge settled the dispute by distributing $108,322.90 of the contained $253,000, which was about $26.00 per soldier.

The treasury then contained $144,700. In Washington on May 4, Capt Micajah Clark, Acting Confederate Treasurer distributed $56,116 to various cabinet members, officers, soldiers, and naval personnel. Clark's last payment was $86,000 to Commander James A Semple, CSN for distribution through three different persons in various states. The Confederate treasury was then paid out completely at Washington, GA.

The $450,000 bank assets carried from Richmond had been untouched since April 24, at the Bank of Georgia branch in Washington, GA near the public square. On the morning of May 24, 1865, five wagons with soldiers and bank representatives loaded the bank assets into wagons with the purpose of returning the funds to the original banks in Virginia by what they hoped was the safest route across the Savannah River, to Abbeville, SC for transport by train to Richmond. The loaded wagons arrived near Chennault, GA seventeen miles NNE of Washington after sundown. The entourage made a camp near the home of Reverend Abraham D. Chennault, a prominent Methodist preacher.

Legend has it that near midnight twenty or so men on horseback surprised the sleeping defenders, driving them into the nearby woods for cover from the gunshots. The riders proceeded to the wagons and began to pillage the containers, filling their saddlebags and littering the ground

In this Harper's Weekly engraving, Union soldiers are shown searching for buried Confederate gold on a southern plantation.

with about $40,000 worth of silver and gold coin. The bank officials indicated that $251,029 was stolen and $40,000 was spread on the ground and the $159, 929.90 amount that was not stolen continued on to Abbeville by wagon and then train to Richmond.

When informed of the robbery, ex-Confederate General Edward Porter Alexander recovered approximately $70,000 from the robbers and returned $110,000 to the Bank of Georgia Branch in Washington, GA that included the $40,000 collected on the ground. Return of these funds to the Richmond banks was legally fought by politicians and bankers for many years with the final decision in 1893 by the Court of Claims giving $16,987.88 to the banks and $78,276.49 to the Federal Government.

The thieves thus successfully gathered about $179,000. There is no way to verify the individual stories as to what happened to the money. Some treasure hunters still try to use metal detectors in the area nonetheless.

"It should be noted that the weight of $250,000 in silver dollars is 9,555 pounds. From April 8 to May 2, the treasury and bank assets were loaded then unloaded from train cars to wagons, from wagons to train cars, and from wagons to different strange locations at least eleven different times by midshipmen and the other naval guards."[36]

South Carolina honors John C. Calhoun

John C. Calhoun
The Most Recognized Member
Of The Leadership Network

1782 ❧❧ 1850

John Caldwell Calhoun was born on March 18, 1782, in Abbeville District, South Carolina, near Long Cave Creek located in the present-day McCormick County, SC. His parents, Patrick and Martha Caldwell Calhoun were of Scotch-Irish ancestry. The Calhouns had immigrated to Pennsylvania during the 1730s and moved south in 1756, reaching the South Carolina back country. Patrick was a prosperous planter in this district. He served in the South Carolina legislature from 1768 to 1774 and during the American Revolution he sided with the patriot cause.

Young John attended a "Field School" for a few months each year. In 1795, he entered a private academy in Appling, Georgia. He had a long course of self-study and also was tutored by Reverend Moses Waddel, a strict Presbyterian minister. During times of school closure, Calhoun was tutored by his sister. Waddel established a prominent academy in 1804 in the Abbeville District. John lost his father at an early age, forcing him to work and complete his studies at the same time. His older brothers, William and James, were successful cotton planters and merchants and helped to finance his education.

John entered Yale College at age twenty as a recognized prodigy and graduated Phi Beta Kappa in two years in 1804. As a diligent student he then attended Litchfield Law School in Connecticut, the school attended by other notable students such as James Madison and Aaron Burr. Calhoun then read law in Charleston, SC with a distinguished attorney, William Henry de Saussure. He was admitted to the Bar in 1807, before returning to Abbeville. There he soon found he disliked practicing law and quickly turned his attention to politics, winning election to the SC House of Representatives in 1808. After his term in the state legislature, he became a US Representative from South Carolina with a reputation as a Jeffersonian Republican in Congress.

In 1811, he married his first cousin once removed, Floride Bonneau Colhoun (1792-1866). Floride was born in Charleston, SC, the daughter of US Senator John E. Colhoun and Floride Bonneau. She was a niece of Rebecca Colhoun Pickens, wife of Revolutionary War General Andrew Pickens. The Senator Calhoun was aide-to-camp to his brother-in law, General Pickens. Young Floride would spend summers with the Colhoun family in Newport, RI where she became friends with the Litchfield law student, John C. Calhoun.

John E. Colhoun, the first cousin and father-in-law of John C. Calhoun, also owned land in the upland Pendleton District of South Carolina on a plantation named Twelve Mile. Fort Hill, then known as Clergy Hall, was built in 1803, as the manse for Old Stone Church just a few miles away from Twelve Mile. When Fort Hill came up for sale, Floride's mother purchased the property and expanded its acreage.

John C. Calhoun and Floride Bonneau were married in 1811, on Rice Hope Plantation in the South Carolina Lowcountry of the Cooper River, Bonneau's Ferry, Berkeley County, SC. The couple eventually had ten children, five sons and five daughters. Three of the daughters died in infancy and one had a spinal condition requiring her to be constantly in her mother's care. The youngest daughter,

Anna Maria (1817-1875), was called the brightest child and was later married to Thomas Green Clemson, the founder of Clemson University.

After their wedding John and Floride Calhoun began their marriage on Bath Plantation in McCormick County, SC. Establishing his reputation as a successful planter proved important to Calhoun's political career, however much of the time he left the plantation management in his wife's care while he worked in Washington.

In 1812, Calhoun and Henry Clay of Kentucky, two famous "War Hawks" led the fight to convince the House of Representatives to declare war on Great Britain, (War of 1812) to stop British raids on American shipping. Calhoun worked along with Secretary of State James Monroe to introduce the war bill in Congress that would strengthen the nation's defenses.

Calhoun became Secretary of War under James Monroe from 1817 to 1824. Monroe seemed to have a special fondness for Calhoun and his wife, Floride, who became one of the capitol's most popular hostesses. After the war, Calhoun was responsible for establishing the Second Bank of the US. The Calhoun family moved at this time to her mother's Georgetown, Washington, DC home named Oakley.

In 1824, Calhoun ran for president along with four others: John Quincy Adams, Henry Clay, William H. Crawford from Georgia, and Andrew Jackson. George McDuffie, a Congressman from South Carolina and good friend endorsed his candidacy. Not long into the campaign, Calhoun withdrew from the presidential race and ran for vice president unopposed. Calhoun served as vice president for the US in 1824, under John Quincy Adams and was re-elected in 1828 under Andrew Jackson.

Calhoun was a nationalist at the outset of his political career and at first supported the Tariff Bill of 1828. The so-called

"Tariff of Abominations" included no tax concessions to the benefit of southern agricultural interests while benefiting northern industrialists. Calhoun then changed his opinion on the tax and drafted for the South Carolina legislature his "Exposition and Protest." In this essay, he advocated a state veto or nullification of any federal law that would impinge on the minority interests of a state. While originally the document was published anonymously, it became referred to as Calhoun's Doctrine of Nullification and was presented to the South Carolina House of Representatives.

George McDuffie, the South Carolinian legislator was a prominent member of the SC Nullification Convention in 1832 and like Calhoun became an eloquent champion of state sovereignty while recognizing the possibility and cost of secession.

Armistead Burt, who married Martha Calhoun, a niece of John C. Calhoun, supported Calhoun in his opposition to the 1828 Tariff and was appointed Secretary of the 1832 South Carolina convention, which passed the Ordinance of Nullification declaring the federal tariff null and void.

At the same time as the Tariff Act discussions in Washington, Floride Calhoun, the Second Lady of the United States had become a prominent hostess in Washington. She became best known in 1831 for her leading role in the "Petticoat Affair," which occurred while her husband was Vice President under President Andrew Jackson. Mrs. Calhoun led the Cabinet wives in ostracizing Mrs. Peggy Eaton, the wife of Secretary of War, John Eaton, for her supposedly low moral character. President Jackson defended the Secretary of War and his wife, straining the relationship between the President and Vice President and forcing all of the Cabinet Members to resign. The damage of the "Petticoat Affair" effectively ended any legitimate chance of Calhoun winning the Presidency of the United States.

Calhoun also opposed Jackson on states' rights issues, which led to his resignation as Vice President in 1832. He was the first vice president to resign, but was quickly appointed Senator from South Carolina. For the rest of his life he defended the slave plantation system and opposed Daniel Webster in the Senate on slavery and states' rights.

In 1832, after Calhoun moved to the Senate, Floride returned to live at the Fort Hill Plantation, which had been expanded from the original stone manse, now including extensive acreage. She became the plantation mistress, managing all of the required affairs. In 1836, at the death of her mother and namesake, she inherited the title to Fort Hill. After the death of her husband in 1850, she became the sole owner of the property. Through the years before her death in 1871, she worked to ensure that Fort Hill would become the property of her daughter Anna Maria Calhoun Clemson and her husband Thomas Green Clemson. Floride was buried near her children at the St. Paul's Episcopal Church in Pendleton, SC.

In the Senate, Calhoun joined forces with Henry Clay to create a compromise leading to a revised tariff acceptable to the southern states. From 1844-1845, he served as Secretary of State under President John Tyler, mostly focusing on the annexation of Texas. After Polk was elected President, Calhoun returned to the Senate where he continued for the rest of his life.

Calhoun made trips back to South Carolina and the surrounding states with his friends and political counterparts. He is known to have visited along with Wade Hampton III in Cashiers in 1840-1850, at the McKinney's boarding house.

While living in Washington, he suffered from tuberculosis and was cared for by Armistead Burt, his nephew by marriage and a US Congressman. In 1845, he had a chronic cough and a sputum production from his lungs. He insisted to Burt that he only needed rest. He was next door to Burt in the Hill's boarding house. Still he continued his work for more years. Later he and Burt lived a further distance apart, but Burt continued to visit him daily.

He died in Washington in March 1850, with his son Patrick and a caregiver at his side. In his honor the bells rang out from the St. Phillips and St. Michaels Churches in Charleston, SC. After a funeral service in the Senate, he was taken to St. Phillips Churchyard in Charleston with the gravesite marker of CALHOUN.

It has been recognized that Calhoun along with Daniel Webster, Henry Clay, and Andrew Jackson, dominated political life from 1815 to 1850. He was a gifted speaker and debater, an original thinker in political theory and a person of broad reading. He was especially well read in philosophy, history and contemporary economic and social issues. An acknowledged intellectual of the highest order, Calhoun was a truly gifted American politician.

In 1957, the United States Senators honored Calhoun as one of the five greatest Senators of all time. The John C. Calhoun marble statue in the US Capitol Statutory Hall, along with Wade Hampton III, occupies one of the two niches allotted to South Carolina.

Statue honoring John C. Calhoun in
National Statuary Hall, US Capitol

Bath Plantation

McCormick County, South Carolina

Bath Plantation was located in McCormick County, one mile from the Savannah River in the same area of South Carolina as the Calhoun family homesteads often referred to as Calhoun Falls. After John C. Calhoun's marriage to Floride Bonneau Colhoun in 1811, they made their home at Bath Plantation. Calhoun had already entered politics, representing the Abbeville District in the state legislature beginning in 1808, and in national politics as a US Congressman in 1811. Calhoun left most of the management of the plantation to his capable wife. He did, however, during his tenure as plantation owner, develop a subsoil plow that became widely used by other plantations.

Fort Hill Plantation

Home Of
John C. Calhoun 1825-1850

Thomas Green Clemson 1872-1888

Fort Hill Plantation located in the Pendleton District, Pickens County, SC was the home of John C. Calhoun, South Carolina's pre-eminent statesman and his wife Floride Bonneau Colhoun. The Calhouns lived part time in the house after receiving it from Floride's mother in 1825. From 1832, until Mrs. Calhoun's death in 1866, Fort Hill was their permanent home. John Calhoun was away from the home serving in Washington, DC in 1850, when he died of tuberculosis.

Fort Hill home of John C. Calhoun, expanded from the
Clergy House by his mother-in-law Floride Bonneau

The house was originally built as a four room house in 1803, by a Presbyterian pastor and was called Clergy Hall. When the Calhoun's received the home they enlarged it to fourteen rooms and renamed it Fort Hill. As typical of the time, the Greek Revival house has two stories supported by four massive columns.

When John Calhoun died in 1850, Floride became the sole owner of the home and its 1341 acres. Through many legal proceedings at the death of family members and finally at auction in 1872, the home and 814 acres was received by Anna Maria Calhoun Clemson, daughter of Floride and John Calhoun and wife of Thomas Greene Clemson. During many of these proceedings, Armistead Burt provided counsel and assistance to Anna Maria and Thomas Clemson.

Thomas and Anna Clemson moved into Fort Hill in 1872, and occupied the home until both of their deaths, Anna in 1875, and Thomas in 1888. At his death, the house and acreage was bequeathed to the State of South Carolina for an agricultural college with the stipulation that the house and furnishings were to be kept in repair and open to the public.

The home was designated a National Historic Landmark in 1960, and is operated as a public treasure by Clemson University.

Gravesite for John C. Calhoun in Charleston, SC

South Carolina honors George McDuffie

George McDuffie
A Recognized Orator
Of The Leadership Network

1790 ❧❧ 1851

George McDuffie was born on August 10, 1790, the son of Scottish immigrants, John and Jane McDuffie in Columbia County, Georgia, three miles from Thomson, GA, in the now named McDuffie County.

Born of modest means, McDuffie's extraordinary intellect was noted while clerking at a store in Augusta, Georgia. James, an older brother of John C. Calhoun, and who recognized the talent sent George to live with another of the Calhoun brothers, William, in the Pendleton District of South Carolina.

In 1807, the Calhoun family sponsored McDuffie's education at Reverend Dr. Moses Waddel's famous Willington Academy. Reverend Waddel was a strict Presbyterian minister and brother-in-law of future statesman John C. Calhoun. His academy was founded in 1804, in Willington, South Carolina in the Abbeville District. It grew to be the most noted prep school in the region, its fame reaching even to distant states. The academy produced many leaders including eleven state governors and dozens of congressmen.

Dr. Waddel required students to memorize on a daily basis long passages from the Greek Classics. Great numbers of his pupils were able to enter the junior class of South Carolina College, Yale, or Princeton. Waddel taught his students to think and participate in weekly debates. After leaving Willington in 1819, Dr. Waddel was instrumental in reorganizing the University of Georgia.

McDuffie later graduated from South Carolina College in 1813, with honors and was admitted to the bar in 1814. He began practicing law in Pendleton, South Carolina and in 1815, moved to Edgefield, SC to become the law partner of congressmen Eldred Simkins. In 1818, George McDuffie was elected to represent the Edgefield District in the South Carolina House of Representatives.

In 1821, he was selected to replace his law partner Eldred Simkins, who declined to run for re-election in the U.S. House of Representatives. George McDuffie won his election to represent the South Carolina 5th Congressional District serving for 13 years until 1834.

In 1820, George McDuffie bought his plantation Cherry Hill located on the Savannah River near Willington, not far from Reverend Moses Waddel's school in the Abbeville District, present day McCormick County. Cherry Hill had first been owned by Major Ezekiel Noble. Throughout his life, McDuffie improved the property and added to the plantation's five thousand acres. The plantation was named for the wild cherries that grew in the area. Cherry Hill Plantation produced cotton on a grand scale during the Golden Age of King Cotton. McDuffie made the plantation his home until his death in 1851.

After his death, McDuffie's friend Armistead Burt, whose Orange Hill plantation adjoined McDuffie's beloved Cherry Hill, eulogized his friend saying:

"Able and graceful as was his written composition, faultless as was his elocution, majestic as was his intellect, it was his eloquence that gave him his great superiority. The speeches of Calhoun were philosophical and grand, the speeches of

> *Webster were logical, massive, and masterly, the speeches*
> *of Clay and Preston were polished and brilliant. But*
> *Greece had but one Demosthenes, Rome one Cicero, and*
> *America has had but one McDuffie.*"[37]

McDuffie entered Congress as a nationalist and supporter of John C. Calhoun. He soon was entangled in the political feud between Calhoun and William H. Crawford of Georgia. In 1822, McDuffie engaged William Cumming from Augusta, GA, a Crawford supporter, in a bitter newspaper battle and the two met for two duels. McDuffie was severely wounded twice. Despite the fact that he survived, McDuffie's wounds lingered. The bullet that hit his back and spinal column contributed to his physical and mental decline in his later years.

During the 1820s, in Congress, McDuffie changed his nationalist position after Congress passed a series of tariffs that he thought harmed South Carolina and unfairly benefited the North. He initiated the fight against federal tariffs, which were imposed on imported goods to protect New England manufacturers. Together with John C. Calhoun, McDuffie developed the doctrine of nullification, which postulated that a state has the right to nullify a federal law with which it disagreed.

This doctrine was put to a test in 1832, when South Carolina had its convention and passed the Ordinance of Nullification. President Andrew Jackson threatened to send troops to the state to enforce the tariff. Militia units were called up and the state braced for war. A national crisis was averted only by a last-minute compromise promoted by Senators John Calhoun of Georgia and Henry Clay of Kentucky that gradually reduced the tariff, but this crisis ultimately led to the state's secession from the Union.

George McDuffie and Mary Rebecca Singleton were married in 1829, in the High Hills of Santee in Sumter District, South Carolina. Mary was the first daughter of Richard Singleton, a good friend of Wade Hampton II spending their summers together in White Sulphur Springs in Virginia. Mary often visited Washington, D.C. and from the gallery watched the proceedings of the U.S. House of Representatives. When she was seen there, McDuffie's friends would say, "The South Carolina orator will be at his best today."

George and Mary had one daughter before Mary died in 1830. Their daughter, Mary Singleton McDuffie, was married to Wade Hampton III in 1858, making George McDuffie the father-in-law of Wade Hampton III.

In 1834, McDuffie resigned from Congress to become Governor of South Carolina. During his time as governor, he helped to reorganize the South Carolina College. In 1843, he was elected to become a United States Senator and held his seat until 1846, when his poor health forced him to retire. He died in 1851, and was buried in the Singleton family cemetery in Wedgefield, Sumter County, South Carolina in the "High Hills of Santee."

McDuffie's life was significant in shaping the major historical events of the antebellum era in American history. His brilliance and oratorical skills prepared him for public service in Congress. He was the most sensational orator of his time. It was said that:

> *"His peculiar style is without a rival. His voice resembles the harsh terrific blast of a trumpet . . . He has power to force open the eyes of men and when open, he can illuminate or blind them. His elocution smites on the popular heart like the club of Hercules."* [37]

Cherry Hill Plantation

George McDuffie Home

The Cherry Hill Plantation was located on the Savannah River in McCormick County, South Carolina adjoining Orange Hill Plantation at Leroy's Ferry. The plantation name was derived from the wild cherries that grew on the land.

George McDuffie purchased the plantation from Ezekiel Noble around 1820. Nobel's home had burned, so McDuffie built a new two story home and expanded the land to include 5000 acres. During his time at the plantation the main crops were cotton, corn and grains.

During McDuffie's long and politically active life he lived and enjoyed his surrounds of the plantation. He made it his home until his death in 1851.

In 1858, the plantation was sold to Charles Lockhart Pettigrew. An historic marker now stands near the entrance to the plantation, though the land is now owned by the US Army Corps of Engineers, McCormick County, SC.

High Hills of Santee

The High Hills of Santee is a region in the western part of Sumter County, South Carolina. Almost 25 miles long and 5 miles wide, this chain of hills is between the coastal plain to the east and north to the Santee River. The region parallels east of the Wateree River, attaining almost mountainous appearance being almost 300 feet above the swampy lowland of the river.

Sumter County was named after Thomas Sumter who came to the region from Virginia in 1767, and with his wife owned and managed a successful plantation. Thomas Sumter was a Brigadier General in the South Carolina militia during the American Revolutionary War and later became South Carolina's US Senator.

The High Hills area in the early 1800s became a popular retreat for the wealthy cotton plantation owners, with a reputation as a pleasant place to spend the summer and escape the heat and malaria from the Lowcountry. Many successful cotton plantations were established in the region by families such as the Broughtons, the Dinkins, the Richardsons, and the Singletons.

Col. Richard Singleton (1776-1852) was from an established family in the High Hills. Col. Singleton was a very close friend of Col. Wade Hampton II. Both shared a keen interest in the breeding and racing of horses. The Singleton and Hampton families summered together in the mountains at White Sulphur Springs, VA.

In the High Hills, Col. Singleton had his Melrose Plantation on the Wateree River near the town of Wedgefield. His oldest daughter, Mary Rebecca Singleton was born in 1805, and was married in 1829 to Congressman George McDuffie at family owned Midway Plantation, also in

Sumter County. Their daughter, Mary Singleton was married to Wade Hampton III in 1858. Col. Singleton's daughter, Angelica was married to Abraham Van Buren. She served as the mistress of the White House in Washington during the administration of her father-in-law, President Martin Van Buren.

Through the years many of the southern leaders enjoyed the High Hills of Santee as residents and guests. George McDuffie found the area so pleasant that he asked to be buried there in the graveyard at Melrose Plantation.

Some of the notable residents of this area of South Carolina were:

1734 – Thomas Sumter, early settler and Revolutionary War general

1755 – Richard Furman, Baptist minister, founder of Furman University

1779 – Joel Roberts Poinsett, statesman and scientist for which the Pointsettia was named

1816 – John L. Manning, owner of Millford Plantation and Governor of South Carolina

1823 – Mary Boykin Chestnut, author of *A Diary from Dixie*, was born in Statesburg.

*Gravestone of George McDuffie at Melrose Plantation
in the High Hills of Santee, SC*

Thomas Green Clemson honored in South Carolina

Chapter 5

Thomas Green Clemson

A Leader In Education
for the Leadership Network

1807 ❦ 1888

very sincerely,
Th. G. Clemson

Thomas Green Clemson IV was born in Philadelphia on July 1, 1807, the third of six children of Thomas Green Clemson, III, a prosperous merchant, and Elizabeth Baker. In 1813, his father died and his father's second cousin John Gest was appointed guardian over Thomas and his five siblings. Thomas was a beneficiary of his father's $100,000 life savings, which was split between him and his five siblings.

Clemson studied in schools in Philadelphia and from 1823-1825, was educated at a military academy in Vermont, also known as Norwich University. Early in his life, he developed an intense interest in chemistry. He continued his education in Paris, attending lectures at the Sorbonne Royal College and earning a diploma as an assayer from the Royal School of Mines in 1831, in Paris.

With the certification of a mining engineer and assayer, he was a very successful engineer consulting on projects in Paris, Philadelphia, and Washington. His very large practice included determining the value of the minerals found in mines. For a short time, he operated John C. Calhoun's gold mine at Dahlonega, GA. Meanwhile, he wrote many excellent articles on the study of science and engineering, which were published in scientific journals.

When Clemson met Anna Maria Calhoun, the eldest and favorite daughter of John C. Calhoun of SC, he changed his mind about being a confirmed bachelor. They were married in 1838, at Fort Hill, Calhoun's plantation in Pendleton, SC. Clemson became a very close friend of his father-in-law as both had a great interest in farming and politics.

In 1844, President John Tyler appointed Clemson as the highest-ranking American diplomat to Belgium, where he served until 1851. The Clemsons were very popular abroad. Clemson spoke several languages, including French and German. He was a brilliant conversationalist and in demand at parties and celebrations. Because of his education, historians have called Clemson "a quintessential 19th century Renaissance man." In his court attire, he showed off his six foot-six inch height with his weight about 200 pounds and his size fourteen shoes. He played the violin very well and developed a recognized skill at painting. Later he and his wife showed great skills at acquiring fine paintings for the exhibitions in Belgium and at the Corcoran Art Gallery in Washington, DC.

In 1843, the Clemsons purchased a 1000 acre plot near Anna's home in Edgefield District, SC. The river front property was dense with canes, which Clemson used to study. He also purchased a smaller home in Maryland to be close to resources to facilitate his research and experiments. Clemson later sold the Canebrake Plantation as it became burdensome to make it profitable.

From 1853 to 1861, the Clemsons lived in Maryland near Washington, D.C. where Clemson became a leading agricultural chemist. There he helped organize the Maryland Agricultural College now the University of Maryland. In 1859, the Secretary of the Interior appointed Clemson as Superintendent of Agricultural Affairs. A significant progress in agriculture documentation and improvements took place under his leadership.

When the threat of Civil War became eminent, he resigned his US post and returned to South Carolina. In 1861, Clemson enlisted in the Confederate Army and was assigned to the Army of the Trans-Mississippi Department, serving in Arkansas and Texas developing nitrate mines for explosives. After the war, the Clemsons lived in South Carolina either at Pendleton, SC or at her mother's Fort Hill Plantation.

Clemson's life showed his strong belief that the South needed improved agricultural and scientific education. It was his main idea in life. Fort Hill became the property of the Clemsons in 1871, from the estate of Anna's mother Floride Calhoun. Mrs. Calhoun survived her husband John C. Calhoun by over 20 years. At the time of her mother's death in 1871, all of Thomas and Anna's four children had died. In 1875, Anna Clemson died suddenly. These deaths were terrible blows to Thomas Clemson, who became a lonely old man. Letters from him to Armistead Burt showed his depression. Burt and Clemson had visited with each other frequently because of their marriage to the members of the Calhoun family and the proximity of Fort Hill to Abbeville and to Cashiers, NC.

Clemson died on April 6th, 1888, and was buried in St. Paul's Episcopal churchyard in Pendleton. He left 814 acres of land and more than $80,000 in assets to the state of South Carolina in his will for the college he envisioned. The state accepted the bequest in 1889 to establish Clemson Agricultural College, now Clemson University in Clemson, South Carolina.

Fort Hill home on Clemson Campus is now open to the public

Thomas Green Clemson statue in front of Tillman Hall,
Clemson University

"The Will of Thomas Green Clemson forever altered
South Carolina state history.
The future of Clemson University is rooted in its past,
back to the days when Thomas Green Clemson and his wife
Anna Calhoun Clemson called Fort Hill their home. It was
in this house that they dreamed of a high seminary for learning
for South Carolina. What began as discussions between a
husband and wife in this historic house has grown into one of
the nation's leading public universities."[39]
—Clemson University

Clemson University

The Dream of
Anna Calhoun Clemson and Thomas Green Clemson

The Clemson story

Clemson was founded in 1889 through a bequest from Thomas Green Clemson, a Philadelphia-born, European-educated engineer, musician and artist who married John C. Calhoun's daughter, Anna Maria, and eventually settled at her family plantation in South Carolina. A longtime advocate for an agricultural college in the Upstate, Clemson left his home and fortune to the state of South Carolina to create the institution that bears his name.

In November 1889, Gov. John Peter Richardson signed a bill accepting Clemson's gift, which established the Clemson Agricultural College and made its trustees custodians of Morrill Act and Hatch Act funds, federally provided for agricultural education and research purposes by federal legislative acts.

Initially an all-male, all-white military school, Clemson Agricultural College opened in July 1893 with 446 students. Clemson became a coeducational, civilian institution in 1955 and was the first traditionally white institution in South Carolina to desegregate since Reconstruction. With academic offerings and research pursuits, the institution became Clemson University in 1964.

From Clemson.edu./history[40]

Wade Hampton III honored
in North Carolina near Cashiers

Wade Hampton III

A Leader Of Military And Political Strength

1818 ❦ 1902

truly sincerely '74
Wade Hampton

Confederate General Wade Hampton III, later Governor of South Carolina and U.S. Senator, was one of the most famous and revered South Carolinians in the nineteenth century. His statue in the U.S. Capitol Statuary Hall was selected by the South Carolina in 1929 to stand with John C. Calhoun as their only two representatives.

Wade Hampton III's father and grandfather should be considered to be generational founders of the Armistead Burt network of influential South Carolinians.

Wade Hampton I (1751-1835)

Hampton's grandfather was a trader, planter, and soldier. In the Revolutionary War, Colonel Hampton lead a brilliant cavalry charge at Eutaw Springs on the Santee River. Later he was promoted to General and deployed to New Orleans.

In 1786, he built the Woodlands plantation near the new state capitol of Columbia. He was elected to the Congress twice while owning and managing plantations in South Carolina, Mississippi, and Louisiana. He was known for his love of horses, raising and racing stallions on tracks around the South. At the time of his death in 1835, he was considered one of the wealthiest men in America.

Wade Hampton II (1791-1858)

Hampton's father was also a soldier, legislator and renowned agriculturist. His work in developing new sustainable turf earned him the name "greatest turfman" in South Carolina. He was educated at Waddel's Willington Academy and also South Carolina College.

He served as a lieutenant in the War of 1812. After the American victory in the Battle of New Orleans, General Andrew Jackson ordered Hampton to take the victory news to President Madison in Washington, DC. Hampton famously rode one horse 750 miles in ten days to his home in Columbia, SC. From there he went to the US capitol by boat to deliver the good news.

Hampton II assisted his father in expanding the Hampton holdings in sugar plantations in Louisiana and cotton farming in Mississippi, as well as a new tract of land called Millwood near the family home of Woodlands. During his lifetime he served as an aide to several South Carolina governors and was elected to the state senate. For more than thirty years, he played an influential role in South Carolina politics.

Wade Hampton III (1818-1902)

Like his father and grandfather, Hampton III was the epitome of the Southern gentleman. He even surpassed them as an equestrian, sportsman, military and political leader. His strength and endurance was legendary. He was a master of five plantations, growing and processing sugar in Louisiana, growing cotton in Mississippi and his home state of South Carolina, excelling in crop rotation and the breeding of horses and cows.

Hampton entered the freshman class at South Carolina College at age fourteen, graduating in 1836, and continuing to read law for two more years. He used his legal knowledge in the improved managing of his vast holdings of plantations, crops, and livestock.

Although he left school at such an early age, his education did not end, as he was a voracious reader. Many years later, he and another member of Congress were discussing the Latin poet Horace and could not agree upon a quotation. When the original was consulted, it was found that Hampton with his classical education and constant reading, had quoted the disputed passage exactly as written.

Wade both wrote well and was a noted orator in his day. When the Hampton home was burned during the Civil War, one of the finest libraries in South Carolina went up in flames, as did many of his writings and collections of rare and exquisite curios and paintings.

He joined Richland County's first Cavalry Company and with his six foot stature and superb riding ability, presented well at military parades. In 1852, he was elected to the House of Representatives in South Carolina and in 1856, to the state Senate, serving until his resignation in 1861.

Hampton was married to Margaret Preston Hampton (1818-1852) from Abington, VA in 1838, when they were both twenty years of age. Five children were born to the marriage with two dying in childbirth. After the death of Margaret Preston in 1852, Hampton remained a single parent until his marriage in 1858, to Mary Singleton McDuffie (1830-1874). Mary was the daughter of South Carolina Governor and later Senator, George McDuffie.

In 1855, Hampton purchased property in Cashiers Valley, North Carolina. For many previous years, he had enjoyed riding horses and hunting in the mountains while staying at the stately boarding house of Modecai Zachary in Cashiers. The coolness and splendor of the "Valley" had provided an escape from the heat of his southern lands. His desire to have his own land to build a hunting lodge with rooms for his whole family gave the impetus for him to purchase land for $5 an acre from Alexander Zachary. With his brother, Kit, the land was purchased and a large lodge with several smaller buildings were constructed. The Hamptons operated this tract (now the site of the High Hampton Inn) as a hunting and fishing home plus an experimental farm with cattle driven from the South Carolina plantation.

When the Civil War was declared in 1861, Hampton offered to enlist as a private in the Army, but was made a colonel by Governor Pickens. Newly appointed Col. Wade Hampton advertised for 1000 volunteers to form the Hampton Legion, comprised of six companies of infantry, four troops of cavalry and a battery of artillery, much of it as his own expense. Hampton organized and trained the Legion as well as leading the troops in the first Battle of Manassas in Virginia in the summer of 1861. Col. Hampton was wounded when a bullet grazed his head and later suffered four more years of battle inflicted wounds.

In 1862, Hampton became a General in the reorganized cavalry division and remained in the cavalry leadership until war's end. As an expert horseman, a skilled swordsman, and a crack shot with pistol and rifle, he was fearless in battle. Wade Hampton took command of the cavalry of Robert E. Lee's Army of Northern Virginia in 1864, when General J.E.B. Stuart was killed. From that moment he never lost a battle.

He was an audacious warrior who led his men from the front with the command "Charge them, my brave boys, charge them!" at Trevillian Station, Virginia as he spurred his horse toward the dismounted Federal troops. Through the end of the War, he received five serious wounds from rifle shots and saber cuts. Hampton surrendered with General Joesph Johnston's Army in North Carolina two weeks after Appomattox.

At the end of Civil War, Hampton was no longer a man of great means. He had lost most of his money and land partially by the debt placed on the land used to fund the military effort and partially by the Union troops burning of all the cash crops. By the end of 1868, his financial situation had become untenable. At the beginning of the War he had owned by his own estimates some 12,000 acres of profitable crops.

Overall, Hampton had written over twenty letters to Armistead Burt and regarded him as his lawyer, valuing Burt's judgment and consultation. Burt had been a long term Hampton family friend and was called his "intimate, political confidant." Hampton wrote in 1868, "It has been very repugnant to take benefit of the Bankruptcy Act, but there seems no choice left to me."

On Christmas Eve, 1868, in Jackson, MS, Wade Hampton filed a petition for bankruptcy for a total debt of his Mississippi interests of an astronomical $1,012, 328.

Hampton also wrote a letter to Burt inviting him to join him in his visits to both "Springs" in Virginia, especially the one in Dagger Springs in western Virginia near Natural Bridge and Lexington. He continued to converse with friends and conclude business while enjoying the cool summers and relaxed surroundings in the Cashiers Valley hunting lodge. As new ventures into profitable businesses, Hampton founded the Southern Life Insurance Company in Atlanta and was also Vice President of the Carolina Life Insurance Company.

During Reconstruction, government officials of South Carolina were first appointed by the Federal government with no residency requirements or oversight of their actions. Federal troops were stationed in South Carolina ensuring that many African Americans could become newly elected officials. Communicating through letters with old friends was a comforting way of remembering better times and hoping for a happy, though very different future.

In 1872, the Amnesty Act was passed by the US Congress restoring the voting and election rights to the officers and soldiers who had served the Confederacy in the Civil War. This gave Hampton and many others the right and opportunity for the first time in seven years to actually influence the election of representatives and for Hampton to serve his state again in an elected position.

It has been reported that Hampton consulted with his brother Kit Hampton and Armistead Burt as to the possibility of standing for his party's nomination for the office of governor of South Carolina. The Hampton brothers spent time at the lodge in Cashiers weighing on the decision and choosing that Wade Hampton should run.

While a hard fought election and a protracted fight to maintain control of the governorship, in April 1876, Wade Hampton III became the first Governor of South Carolina after Reconstruction. He was called by many as the "savior of the state." He wrote to Burt, "We have won a great victory, but we shall have to force great responsibilities and arduous duties."

Hampton was re-elected easily on November 6, 1878. The morning following the election he decided to join friends on a deer hunt and suffered a compound fracture of his lower leg. The wound became infected and after several months the leg had to be amputated.

During his long illness and recovery, Wade both resigned the governorship and was elected by the state legislature to serve as the U.S. Senator beginning in March 1879, for the next twelve years. While it might be a legend that Wade Hampton had a "cork leg" it was no legend that one of the

*Statue of Wade Hampton III in National Statuary Hall,
Washington, DC*

strongest leaders ever from South Carolina was back in the influence for his state.

Many tragedies befell the man who served his beloved state and country throughout his lifetime, including the loss of his family homes, especially late in life in 1899, as arsonists burned Southern Cross and Millwood to the ground with almost no remains. At this time in his life he was often without financial resources, but never without friends. After the loss of this home, the community of friends and admirers came together and built for their elder statesman a new small home in town. On April 11, 1902, Wade Hampton III died. His funeral was the largest ever held in South Carolina with 20,000 mourners, black and white, who lined the streets of Columbia to honor the man who had contributed so much to the state that he loved.

Wade Hampton III gravestone,
Trinity Episcopal Church, Columbia, SC

Millwood Plantation
Columbia, South Carolina

The Hampton family home named Millwood began as a wooded tract across the Garner's Ferry Road from the very large Hampton family tract and home of Woodlands. In 1817, a two-story cottage was built while plans were created for a larger home.

In the 1830s, Wade Hampton II engaged the services of Nathaniel Potter from Rhode Island to renovate and enlarge the home in the Greek Revival style of architecture with six imposing tall fluted pillars with a two-story piazza running across the front.

East of Columbia near the banks of the Congaree River, Millwood and its five acres of gardens became the center of social and political life for the Hampton family and their many friends. Most of the feasts included quality meats and vegetables produced in their own fields. The massive library required two rooms and was always open to guests.

Millwood along with other Hampton homes of Diamond Hill and Woodlands, all near Columbia, were burned in February, 1865, at the same time that General Sherman's Union troops were marching through South Carolina with much destruction in their wake. The property consisting of the ruins left after the burning by the troops was placed on the National Register of Historic Places in 1871. Five of the iconic columns covered in vines serve as a ghostly reminder of those towering figures in South Carolina history, the three Wade Hamptons.

The ruins of the Hampton home at Millwood Plantation

Wade Hampton Hunting Lodge
Cashiers, North Carolina

Wade Hampton III with his brother Kit Hampton came to the green valley of North Carolina in search of recreational activities, escaping the heat and malaria prone summers of South Carolina. The Hamptons were attracted to the beauty and exquisite landscape of Cashiers Valley, describing it as a "paradise." He customarily made the trek with a substantial entourage from South Carolina to his family's seven-bedroom mountain home.

In September 1855, the Hamptons purchased land parcels totaling 400 acres in Jackson County, North Carolina. Hampton and his brother immediately began work on building the lodge, fostering the hunting activities and creating an experimental farm, driving a herd of prize cattle from South Carolina.

The original hunting lodge stood on the property and continued as a summer family hunting home. It was later owned, loved and enlarged by Wade Hampton's niece, Caroline Hampton and her husband Dr. William Halsted from Johns Hopkins Hospital in Baltimore. Dr. Halsted expanded the acreage to 2200 acres and named the property High Hampton. After their deaths in 1922 the property was sold to the McKee family to operate as the High Hampton Inn, a prominent mountain resort. The original lodge house stood on the property until a fire destroyed it in 1932.

Wade Hampton hunting lodge built circa 1856

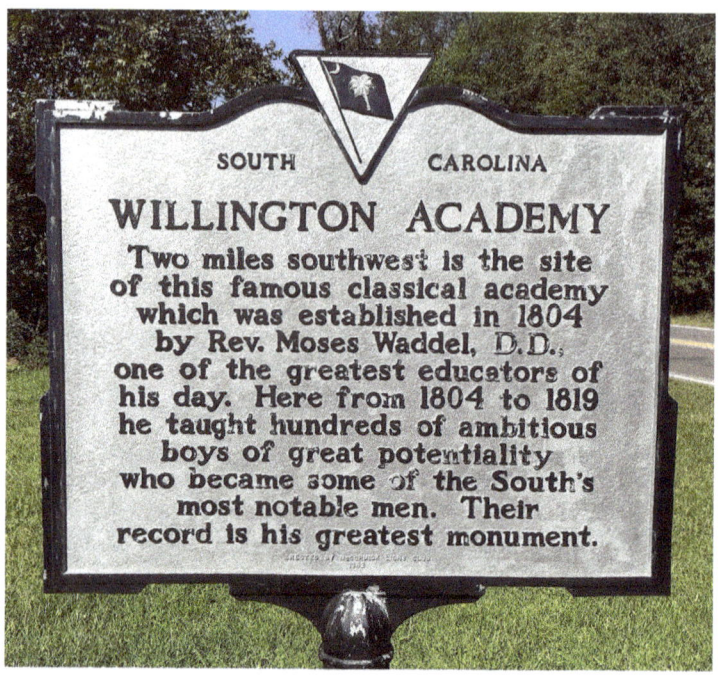

SOUTH   CAROLINA

WILLINGTON ACADEMY

Two miles southwest is the site
of this famous classical academy
which was established in 1804
by Rev. Moses Waddel, D.D.,
one of the greatest educators of
his day. Here from 1804 to 1819
he taught hundreds of ambitious
boys of great potentiality
who became some of the South's
most notable men. Their
record is his greatest monument.

South Carolina honors Moses Waddel

Moses Waddel

A Southern Educator
For The Leadership Network

1770⁓1840

M oses Waddel was born in North Carolina in 1770, and at an early age began teaching future leaders of the South. He graduated from Hampden-Sydney College in Virginia in 1791, where he received a degree and also became licensed to preach by the Presbytery.

It was common at that time for ministers to associate with an academy or college preparatory school. The most famous of these academies was that of Dr. Moses Waddel, which was founded in upcountry Willington, South Carolina in 1804, near the Savannah River. This "Presbyterian Academy," later called Willington Academy, became known throughout the South and was called "Eton in the Woods." The academy was located near the Waddel home on the Orange Hill Plantation.

This school trained the future elite of Georgia and South Carolina with a strict classical education. The graduates generally entered a university at the junior year. Students were required to memorize, translate, and recite two-hundred-fifty lines daily of the original writings in Greek, Latin, and Hebrew. The record for recitation was held by future South Carolina governor and senator George McDuffie who once recited 2,212 lines of Horace.

In 1795, Moses Waddel married Catherine Calhoun, the older sister of John C. Calhoun, who had been tutored by Dr. Waddel. Catherine lived only one year following their marriage, but it was enough time for young John Calhoun to become attracted to Waddel as a teacher.

According to the book *The Great Doctor Waddel* by Dr. James McLeod, the list of students from Waddel's school included two U.S. Vice-Presidents, three Secretaries of State, three Secretaries of War, one assistant Secretary of War, one U.S. Attorney General, Ministers to France, Spain, and Russia, one U.S. Supreme Court Justice, eleven governors, seven U.S. senators, thirty members of the US House of Representatives, twenty-two judges, eight college presidents, seventeen editors of newspapers or authors, five members of the Confederate Congress, two bishops, and three Brigadier Generals.[39]

Five South Carolina governors in a row were his students. In the presidential election of 1828, the winning President and Vice President were both South Carolinians who had studied under Waddel: Andrew Jackson and John C. Calhoun.

Dr. Waddel continued to lead the Willington Academy until he left in 1819, to become the fifth president of the University of Georgia in Athens. He was also the founding pastor of the First Presbyterian Church of Athens, Georgia. He stayed at the University of Georgia for ten years and saw it grow from seven students to over one hundred. After his move to Athens, the Orange Hill plantation was sold to Armistead Burt of Abbeville.

His son, Dr. John Waddel (1812-1895) was one of the organizers of the University of Mississippi and after the Civil War became the chancellor there for about 10 years. He was also a Presbyterian minister.

Dr. Waddel suffered a stroke in 1836, and died in 1840.

Southern Leadership Network
The Letter Routes

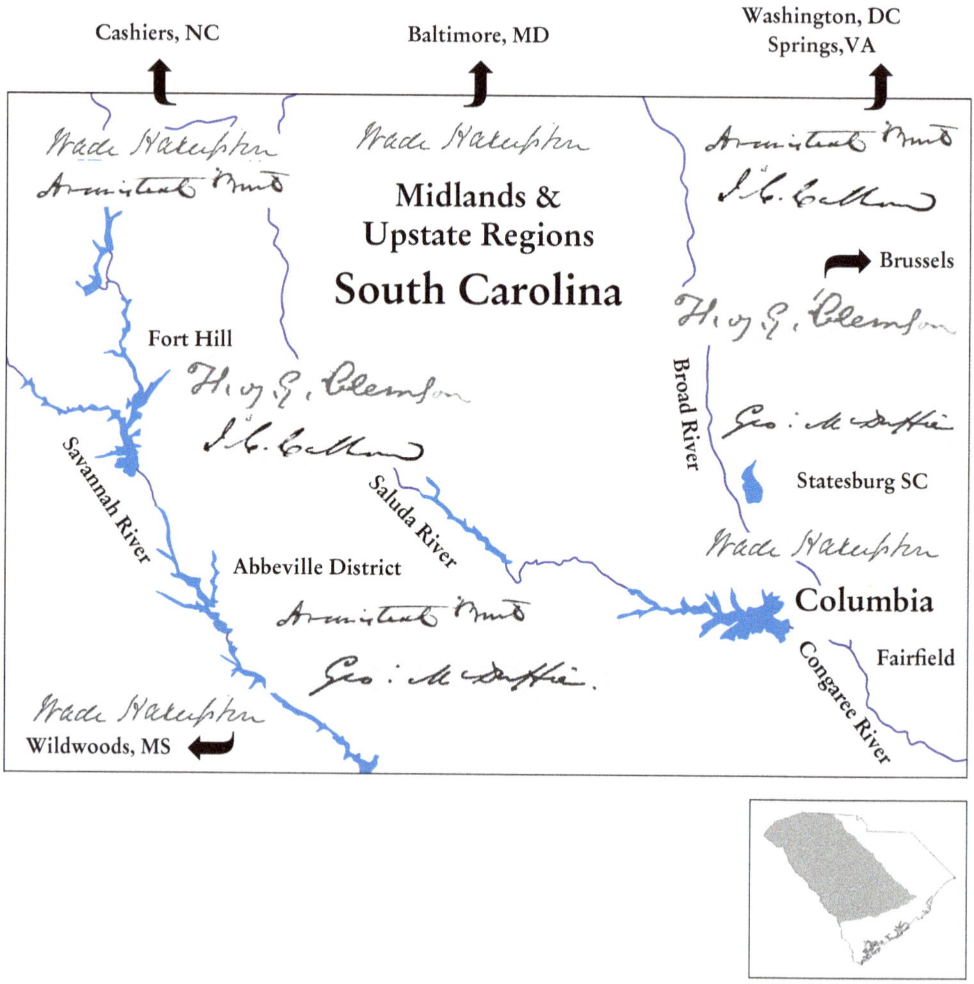

Cashiers, NC

Baltimore, MD

Washington, DC
Springs, VA

Wade Hampton
Armistead Burt

Wade Hampton

Midlands &
Upstate Regions
South Carolina

Armistead Burt
J.C. Calhoun

Brussels

Fort Hill

H. of G. Clemson
J.C. Calhoun

H. of G. Clemson

Geo. McDuffie

Statesburg SC

Broad River

Savannah River

Saluda River

Abbeville District

Armistead Burt

Geo. McDuffie

Wade Hampton

Wade Hampton

Columbia

Fairfield

Wildwoods, MS

Congaree River

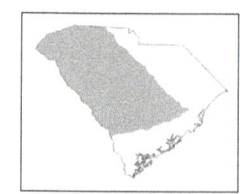

Selected letters between the leaders of Armistead Burt's Southern Leadership Network

The archiving of these letters from the 1800s has been the purview of many researchers and are shared by individuals and three southern universities.

Washington
27. July. 1853.

My dear Sir,

I have drawn a paper, to be
submitted to the President, in your behalf
which I will have signed by some of
your friends, to-morrow. I should like
you to see if it embraces all the points
you wish stated, and besides, I desire
you to indicate the person to whom
it should be delivered when I leave
the city.

I have made my arrangements
to leave the city for South Carolina
to-morrow night, and suppose that
you had better come to the city to-morrow

Sincerely yours
Armistead Burt.

Mr. Clemson.

Letter from Burt to Clemson, 1853

Letters from Armistead Burt

Letters from
Armistead Burt to John C. Calhoun

1 Abbeville Court House, September 19, 1842

Having yielded my own views and inclinations to the desires of many citizens of Edgefield and Abbeville that I should be a candidate for Congress in the place of Mr. Francis W. Pickens...I have heard with much concern, that it has been represented to you...that my feelings towards you personally are not kind...and that I do not concur in the desire...to effect your elevation to the Presidency....and I trust the whole Country will call you...and any contribution within my power to promote it.

...on another subject...General George McDuffie ....thought it advisable to hold a public meeting ...to adopt anti-tariff resolutions...the District is aroused...but we propose measures of mildness and moderation.

2 Hamburg, SC, November 24, 1845

I have written to my Overseer, Mr. Palmer, to let you have my carriage horses....I will be glad to hear by letter addressed to me at Washington City.

I shall...take for granted that you will go to the Senate. The necessity of your doing so has been made apparent and imperative by the late revelations from the Cabinet.

3 Salt Sulphur Springs, VA, September 14, 1846

I have been delayed, a week on account of General George McDuffie...(having) chill and fever for several days. I urged him to go to the Hot Springs...I never saw a greater improvement in a few days. He has been exempt for ten days from all nervous affections...Dr. Thomas Goode ...believes that it is dyspepsia alone.

Our arrangement is to leave the Red Springs the 21ˢᵗ to be in Pendleton about the first of October. I have heard but little news...as there are but few persons of intelligence at the Springs and very few Democrats....the Whigs of this State are very friendly to you-and greatly prefer you to any other Democrat. I am convinced...it will be fatal to the Whigs as well as the Democrats in the South to go into a national Convention...the nominee of each party will be selected with reference to his ability to carry the States of New York and Pennsylvania...This at one blow strikes down all Southern allies.

4 Calhoun's Mill, SC, August 17, 1847

I had received ..a letter from Henry W. Connor of Charleston on the subject of a paper for Washington. A meeting will be held at the Abbeville Court House and I will make an address. As a means of uniting the South and preparing it for resistance, I am disposed to think a paper at Washington will be useful and important. Resistance is our policy as well as our duty.

The Mexican War presents ...a phase of deep and exciting interest and topics for much conversation.

I am pleased to hear that your crop is good. Mine was very fine until the first of August, but has been materially injured by the excessive rains. I have never known such torrents to fall from the clouds. The rain was constant until ten days ago.

5 Willington, SC, November 4, 1848

*Eugenia Calhoun is to be married to Dr. Edwin Parker
the 18th of this month, and Martha Calhoun Burt joins me
in the desire that you and Mrs. Floride Colhoun Calhoun
.....should be present. I have no news but what you have seen
in the papers.*

*The Mexican War is assuming a grave and interesting
aspect. God only knows when and at what cost of blood and
treasure it will end. Colonel Arthur P. Hayes writes for my
advice as to his being a candidate for the Senate.*

*The injury to my cotton exceeds my worst apprehensions.
I did not believe that so much damage could be done by hail. I
shall not make more than twenty five bales.*

Letters from
Armistead Burt to Thomas Clemson

Detailed account of last days of John C. Calhoun
sent to son-in-law Thomas Clemson

1 Washington, May 20, 1850

*Information from the United States will have informed
you that Mr. Calhoun's death occurred before your letter
could have reached me. I did not receive it until the fortnight
after this sad event. I have been very much indisposed ever
since, and too much overcome by it to trust myself with an
attempt to write you about the illness and last moments
of one whose loss is so heavy a bereavement to his whole
country and such affliction to his friends and relatives.*

*On our way to this city, before a meeting of Congress,
we met Mr. Calhoun in Charleston, as I thought, in his usual
health. I thought it quite as good as I could have expected,
and better than when I last saw him. His complexion was
good, and he appeared to have borne the fatigue of the
travel well. We were at the Hotel together, and talked of our
arrangements for the winter. I submitted that matter to him,
and Martha. Mr. C. finally determined to go on Capitol Hill,
and took lodgings at Niles' boarding house. He believed it
would be best for him, as it would save the ascent from the
avenue to the Capitol, which he believed had injured him
last winter. I earnestly advised against it, but without avail.
Martha was so much opposed to going on the Hill, that we
remained on the Avenue all winter. For the first time, we
were thus unfortunately separated. His health remained
quite good, until he took a cold, which affected him very
much. Of this he became much relieved but was quite feeble,
when he determined to attend the sittings of the Senate. I
observed he coughed more than usual, and his expectations
were more frequent and copious, than formerly. A visit to*

93

the Senate when he was quite too feeble to leave his lodgings, and the excitement of debate, threw him back and produced slight fever. I did not regard it as serious, and did not doubt he would recover. He thought, he would soon recover, and I had always found him so calm and accurate an observer of his situation, that my opinion was, in a degree, influenced by his own. Dr. Hall, his Physician, believed he would recover, but advised that he should leave Washington, as soon as he had the strength enough to travel. He was opposed to it, but finally yielded to my entreaties, and consented to go to Mr. Cralle's, his old friend, at Lynchburg, in Virginia. He sent one of his trunks. I saw he did not improve as fast as I expected, and consulted him about the propriety of writing for Mrs. Calhoun. He insisted he was gaining every day, slowly, and strenuously opposed my writing. About two weeks before his death I determined to write Mrs. C. without letting him know it, and did so, asking her to come without delay. But even then I had no fear of his death. But I observed him closely, seeing him from twice to three times in the day and night, and could not see that he was gaining strength, as he thought he was. Three days before his death, I was violently attacked with fever, and saw him no more. Dr. Hall reported to me that he was slowly improving, and I neither knew nor heard, to the contrary, until half hour before he expired. Martha had gone home on a hasty visit and was absent also. Everything that skill or kindness could effect was done. I had procured an excellent and faithful female nurse. Indeed nothing was omitted. His death came upon him unexpected, and from all I heard, he was not aware of its approach until about an hour before he ceased to live. But he died, as quietly as an infant sleeps. The sensation which his death produced, can never be imagined, in Congress and throughout the country. No American, whatever was his station, had higher honor paid to his memory. The whole nation not only mourned, but wept his loss. I send a few of the many tributes

to his virtues and his character which were called forth. I
have no more. Martha's health has been seriously affected by
her grief. Martha sends her love to yourself, Mrs. Clemson,
and the children, with mine. Martha begs that I shall add a
word more to Mrs. Clemson. She says that she did not forget
the miniatures of Mr. Calhoun which Mrs. C. asked her to
have painted this winter. But that Mr. Calhoun said he could
not have it done well here, and that Mrs. Clemson must have
it painted from the one she has in Brussels. She hopes Mrs.
C. will believe that the miniatures were not neglected by her,
and that Mrs. C. will not be disappointed on account of it.

2 Washington, February 10, 1853

I received a letter from Col. Pickens this morning
including a letter to the Honorable Mr. Atherton who was
recently elected to the Senate from New Hampshire and is a
particular friend of General Price. Col. Pickens tells us he
may have some information to give to Atherton rather than
General Price. I have forwarded Col. Pickens letter to Mr.
Atherton as suggested and think is proper and he should
receive it as soon as possible. I have not been out of my room
since I wrote...but should in a day or two will be happy in
doing anything for you.

3 Washington, July 27, 1853

I have a paper to be submitted to the President in your
behalf, which I will have signed by some of your friends
tomorrow. I would like you to see if it embraces all the
points, and besides, I desire you to indicate the persons
to whom it should be delivered when I leave town. I have
made my arrangements to leave the City for South Carolina
tomorrow night, and suppose that you should come to the
city tomorrow.

4 Abbeville, March 31, 1874

*I regret very sincerely that the demands of my
professional business will deny me the pleasure of being at
Fort Hill, tomorrow. I feel sincerely the propriety of going
to Washington to present the memorial of the Tax Payer and
could not forego the higher claims of clients.*

5 Abbeville, September 23, 1876

*I am gradually but steadily regaining my health and
although feeble am doing something in my office. I am sorry
to hear that you are suffering from inflammation of the eyes,
as it severely limits your reading and then increases your
loneliness. I hope, however that it will soon pass off and
that your improved health will enable you to take exercise in
the open air on horseback or otherwise, which I believe will
be greatly beneficial. Our knowledge of the laws of nature
is so limited and yet discoveries are wonderful making it
difficult to say which should be rejected as contrary to science
or reason. This will send us to accept the law of human
theory that all which is contrary to human experiences is to
be rejected as contrary to the law of nature and therefore
incredible.*

*In Abbeville and the adjoining counties there is a great
political excitement for the Democrats to capture a triumph
at the election. The presence and speeches of General
Hampton have excited much enthusiasm wherever he has
gone.*

6 Abbeville. November 10, 1876

I have considered the matter about your overseer and advise that you settle with him without a suit even though you should lose something. You should not have a suit with anyone that you can possibly avoid.

We have carried the elections in Abbeville and the United States and I think Hampton is certainly elected. The election of all our states officers is not so certain as that of Hampton who was ahead of the party vote all over the state. The latest counts show Hampton about 5000 ahead of Chamberlain. It is believed that we will have a majority in the Legislature... of that I am doubtful. If Hampton be elected and Tilden be President we shall have saved the country and especially South Carolina. But we have done nothing of the greatest importance in the state. We have finally settled the relations between the white and colored races without which we could not have had prosperity soon.

7 Abbeville, March 25, 1880

...calling my attention to the News and Courier *of Charleston and my own letter to the Mayor of the city and the proceeding of the City Council in relation to your communications to Simonds and others. I observed that three gentlemen had appeared before the Council and communication will be published thereafter and that Dr. Rose appointing a committee to the arrangements for the removal of the remains of Mr. Calhoun had been rescinded by the Council. I presume that the remains will not be removed and that the City Council and the citizens of Charleston will retain them and erect the monuments. I was in Washington when Mr. Calhoun's remains were brought to Charleston by a boat in which they were transported and attended by a committee from Charleston. I rode in a carriage to the Bank with Mr. Calhoun's son and I had the impression that the Calhoun family consented to the remains being deposited in Charleston. From your letter to Mayor Courteny, I discover that the family of Mr. Calhoun did not consent to that arrangement, but I must infer from the Court proceedings of the council that evidence has been submitted from some of the relations if not from the immediate family of Mr. Calhoun. I presume the promised publication of this matter submitted to the Council to contain something on that subject. I have always regarded the contributions for the monument as a matter between the committee and the family.*

8 Abbeville, May 22, 1880

I have received and read with sympathy and concern your letter and I am distressed by the utter hopelessness which it expresses of justice on appreciation from mankind, and particularly of the qualities of this State. It is very true that you have been called upon to bare bereavements and misfortunes and that you have experienced disappointments and vexations that surely took the fortitude and patience of the wisest of men, but then you have much gratitude of many of us to sustain you. You have had ordinary good health, domestic happiness, and you must have a fortune and tried and true friends. You feel no dependence upon the world, and much but voluntary and limited social intercourse. You have a cultivated mind and you can make books the companions that comfort and console. You must cheer up and abandon to oblivion and forgetfulness the unpleasant experience of the past, as such as its saddening memories. You must learn the somewhat difficult task of flushing and casting away the thorns of life. But you must never despair and struggle with unbroken courage against the ills of life-its nuances and wrongs.

I send herewith the form of an advertisement which is for your purposes. But you must fill up the blanks, with the number of acres, the number of years of the lease and the probably acres of corn, cotton, and other crops. The lease can not be written until you have found a tenant and made a contract with him. The advertisement should be published in papers of large circulation, made in August or September, and I advise that the lease for seven years.

9 Cashiers Valley, September 26, 1880

I have been sick for nearly three weeks but now in better health and hope to be able to leave the Valley for Abbeville. ..have received further correspondence about Mr. Calhoun's remains. I am pleased to know that this climate is impressive to you and I think you should spend the summer in the mountains.

10 Abbeville, May 24, 1881

The mail brought me last night your kind and pleasant note. As Teddy tells me he is going today. I write by him to thank you sincerely for your kindness. I regret that I can not leave home at present as Court is approaching and I must give all the time and health to be in my office quite regularly. I came to the conclusion last summer that Cashiers is too cool for me and I spend but a short time there during the season but as yet I have no plans for the summer. As I write with fingers a little stiff, I send you the most friendly sentiments and grateful kindness.

Letters From Cashiers Valley Neighbor David Norton To Armistead Burt

Franklin, NC, December 25, 1875

Yours of the 11ᵗʰ has come safe to hand the Post Office money order was good, the Postman paid us the money. I sent it to mother. It came in good time for her as she is calculating on letting you have cows next summer. I was sorry to hear about of hard times in your county. Money is scarce in our county. We have had the most pleasant fall and winter I ever saw in my life but some cold....the thermostat was some two degrees. Your place in the Valley was all going right so far.

Jackson County, NC, April 15, 1877

After neglecting for a long time I will attempt writing you. I suppose that you have not received my last letter or you would have written to me before this time. I informed you that I filled your ice house the first time, but since then there has not been any ice to fill it a second time. The snow is 6" at my house today. I do not remember a nicer February and March. Anything that you want done in my line of business, I will try to be ready at any time to work for you.

Washington
27th Oct 1831

My dear Sir,

I have received your letters of the 17 & 19th inst. with their inclosures and am much obliged to you for furnishing me with the statements they contain.

I have little to write. I do not see the least prospect of any satisfactory modification of the Tariff. As far as I can judge from indications, the result will be the repeal of the [...], and the retention of the bounties; that is, the duties will be retained on all articles, the north [...] manufacture, and be repealed on all others. The burden will in its [...] be diminished but the inequality be increased.

J. C. Calhoun

Letter from Calhoun to Burt, 1831

Letters from
John C. Calhoun

Letters from
John C. Calhoun to Armistead Burt

1 Columbia, SC, November 27,1831
I see the Globe *has made Mr. Alexander Speer's last letter the subject of a base attack on me...I can not doubt that it is intended to wage a war on me.....request for help in collecting evidence of Mr. Speer's conversations that were in contradiction to Mr. Speer's letter in the* Globe *which condemned Calhoun...exposure of the base means resorted to by the corrupt corps around the President Andrew Jackson.*

2 Washington, December 27, 1831
I do not see the least prospect of any satisfactory modification of the Tariff...the repeal of the taxes and the retention of the duties on all articles the North can manufacture...it will be taken off the North and left on the South...off the rich and left on the poor...What I write on politicks you will of course understand is not for the publick.

3 Washington, January 16, 1833
We had today the message from Andrew Jackson... Shortly after I took my seat, while the reading was progressing, I perceived that it ought not to pass without a blow...and I accordingly struck...my friends say with great effect on the Senate and the Audience. Our cause looks well... if the Tariff be not adjusted the South will be united in six months.

4 Washington, June 28, 1836
...gratified to learn that my constituents so generally approve of my course. I am of the impression that much has been effected during this session....The bill regulating the deposits and disposing of the surplus ..will do much to restore the ascendancy of the States, and effect a deep political reform.

5 Washington, February 15, 1837

So laborious has been our sittings in the Senate that I have been compelled ...to suspend almost entirely my private correspondence... am not prepared yet to say how far his condemnation of the Carolina Gap (as a route for the proposed Louisville, Cincinnati, and Charleston Railroad) has been warranted by the state of the facts. If it rests on no better foundation than his statement to the Legislature, it is worth nothing.

6 Washington, October 15, 1837

... I shall proceed directly to Abbeville, where I expect to be on the 22nd and glad to see you and also meet with George McDuffie. I trust that McDuffie is right. A national bank now would negatively seal our fate at the South.

7 Washington, January 24, 1838

...My resolutions were taken up, between defending them in the Senate and the more laborious task of correcting and writing out from the most infamous notes. ..every effort to defeat the resolutions, but I succeeded until the 5th Resolution, when I was overpowered by adverse feelings growing mainly out of the presidential controversy. The two prominent candidates with Henry Clay from the South and Martin Van Buren from the North divided the Senate.

8 Fort Hill, November 17, 1838

... I am also of the impression that our true line of policy at Washington at the next session is to shape our course in reference to the finances of the country, which if I do not mistake are reaching an interesting crisis...Revenue ...has been regularly falling off...while the expenditures have been increasing....it follows that one of three things must speedily take place: the Tariff must be renewed; a new debt contracted; or the expenditures be reduced fully one half and that without delay.

9 Washington, February 17, 1839

*...The only political movement of any importance since
I last wrote you was Mr. Henry Clay's on the abolition
question...His speech is far from being sound on many points,
but he has said enough to offend mortally the abolitionists,
which will do much to divide the north and consolidate us...
The prospect is that nothing will be done at this session on
the currency question...There will I think be a great reduction
in the appropriations...a most material point at this time...
the hope that satisfactory readjustment of the Tariff will take
place between this and '42.*

10 Fort Hill, November 2, 1840

*...It is probable that William Henry Harrison will
succeed, and even may by a large vote, but with powerful
minorities in all states, that vote for him. It seems to me,
is we should stand alone, as some absurdly think possible,
we ought to vote for Van Buren; not that he is or ought to
be a favorite, but that it has become a point of honor and
expediency, and the greater the minority, the stronger both.
In any other event, it strikes me, the State ought to vote for
James K. Polk were he a candidate....I understand...that he is
a candidate for reelection as governor of Tennessee....I hope,
that every thing will be done to avoid distraction and to keep
the State quiet and united. If Harrison should succeed our
Union at home may be necessary, not only for the safety of
the South, but of our free institutions. It would be better for
the South to have a monarch at once, than a $50,000,000
bank located in Philadelphia or New York....which would look
to us exclusively as a subject of plunder.*

11 Washington, January 24, 1841

...We are getting along slowly with business, but I am inclined to think, the better for being slow. ...I had hoped ... but the William Henry Harrison leaders in the Senate ...are pushing forward most of their leading measures in order to prepare for a national bank; the repeal of the Subtreasury, the distribution of the proceeds of the sale of publick lands... We are now engaged in a warm discussion of the distribution scheme. I spoke yesterday against the unconstitutional and inequities measure at large and was replied to by Mr. Daniel Webster. The debate is likely to become very warm. If it should succeed, it would be fatal. There is no end to the extent of plunder, which would grow out of it.

12 Fort Hill, September 29, 1842

...I am gratified to learn that you are a candidate for Congress and hope you may succeed. It gives me great pleasure to state... that although I heard rumors that your feelings were not altogether kind towards me, I have never permitted them to have any influence on me. I have written to General George McDuffie on the subject of the meeting to be held in Abbeville...and concur in the views that you throw out. Let the abominable measure be denounced as it ought to be, and the strongest regret expressed that any portion of the party should have given it their vote. ...take good care ...to the great body of the Democratick party ...they are with us... and stood up manfully for free trade.

13 Fort Hill, December 23, 1843

... There is now no doubt, that the political management and political machinery are too strong for the people. They have forced Martin Van Buren on the party against the wishes of three-fourths of the party. I have decided to address my friends and supporters, and to assign my reasons for not permitting my name to go before the Baltimore convention. We have nothing to hope from the two great factions that are now contending for the spoils, they have extorted from us. The leaders of the Democratick portion are more hostile to us, than the Whigs...the object of my address is two fold; to put myself rectus, and the next to afford those, who agree with me a point on which to rally. I have done my duty, it rests with them to do theirs.

14 Fort Hill, Sept 17, 1845

I received several letters from different parts, some expressing their regret that I left the Senate and others pressing my return. My own impression is, that as far as I am personally concerned, I have nothing to gain by returning, while I may lose much for the present...I owe it to myself and the country to be governed by higher considerations. To yield our desires and interest to the good of the country is the essence of patriotism. It would be prudent to abstain from making any remarks from which it might be inferred that you had conversed with me on the subject of returning to the Senate.

15 Fort Hill, September 21, 1847

...I am about to make a movement on the improvement of Savannah river for steam boat navigation. It is a subject of which I have a deep interest. I made a visit...and got my full account of the impediments, which obstruct its navigation... but may be overcome, at an expense mush less than the construction of a railroad... It is true, that we on this side of the State, should look to our interest. The State as yet, has done nothing for us, while it has expended millions in other quarters. I am opposed to her interfering at all, except it can be done by an advance of her credit on some safe security, but, ... ought to insist on an equal share in proportion to our just claims.

16 Fort Hill, September 13, 1849

George McDuffie informs me, that you had a good crop when he left home. I hope it continues so.... The time for leaving for Washington begins to be near at hand. The session cannot but be an important one. Your House of Representatives will be so nearly balanced, that, I think, it will be important, that you and our other members should be on the ground some days before hand. The choice of speaker will be important and difficult to make. I trust our delegation... and in no event to vote for Howell Cobb of Georgia as speaker.

17 Washington November 5, 1849

...I am very desirous, on every account, to be in the same mess (living arrangements) with Martha Calhoun Burt and your self. I would prefer the Hill...in consequences of a regard to my health...but if not, I will join you in the location you suggest, or any other contiguous, rather than separate from you and Martha. I concur as to the caucus, with a modification...To take the ground you suggest, not to go in with those who refused to sign the address, would I fear tend too strongly to divide the South.

Letter from
John C. Calhoun to George McDuffie

Fort Hill, March 9, 1844

No one has greater cause to be distressed by the astonishing events of which your letter conveyed....except the families and the immediate connections f those, who fell by the fatal explosion aboard the U.S.S. Princeton on 2/28. But my loss, as great as it is, is nothing compared to that of the publick, especially the South, and by the death of Mr. Able P. Upshur. No one feel it more, in that respect, aside from our personal relations, than I do, and among other reason, that his death, at this time, should, in your opinion and that of other friends, create a necessity for my returning to public life.

Letters from
John C. Calhoun to Thomas G. Clemson

1 Fort Hill, March 8, 1844

Mr. Calhoun's letter advises Mr. Clemson on financial issues

As to standing, a (law) suit on what you regard as the original bargain, I would by no means advise it; unless your proof is strong...for it would cost you, probably, in the long run a sum equal to the difference, besides the vexation.

You must have a great deal of trouble in commencing your settlement...the country must be singularly destitute of means...distressed to think that you have found it so hard to get ordinary supplies. I know of no other way by which you can get the mail route of which you speak, except by petition on the part of those interested...the Villagers of Edgefield and Newberry and the citizens along the route. The petition ...should be in duplicate; one for your member Armistead Burt and the other to Mr. George McDuffie, Senator from SC.

2 Fort Hill, September 18, 1845

We have had almost one continued drought and sun shine...the streams are all lower than ever remembered... the crops are failing...it will difficult for this and the other Southern Atlantick States to get through the next year... From Alabama I have very favourable accounts. We shall have a very large surplus for sale. My gold mine is yielding moderately. As to politicks, I can say little. I am urged to return to the Senate. My inclination is against it, but the state of our affairs, external and internal, is so critical that I should feel it my duty to serve, if the State should request me. I fear the Oregon question will lead to difficulties with England....in its present entanglement it requires not only great skill and prudence, but great firmness and decision to avoid a conflict between the two countries. I believe she (England) is exceeding desireous, on many accounts, as we ought to be, to avoid a war; yet folly and weakness may force the two countries into deadly conflict.

3 Washington, July 11, 1846

The most important occurrence is the passage of the Tariff bill through the House...its fate in the Senate is doubtful, but I think it will pass. It is clear from the vote of the House, that the days of protection is numbered. If its advocates are wise, they will agree to the best terms they can now get. The South and West have never been so strongly united...in reference to the tariff...but in publick lands and the warehousing policy...my report on the memorial of the Memphis Convention has greatly contributed. With the exception of the Mexican war, the course of events thus far has been more in conformity to my views, than what they have been for many years. I fear the war will not come to a speedy termination and that it will prove very expensive...the wet weather has ceased; and it is now clear and very warm, which is favourable to our Southern crops. Mrs. Calhoun and Mrs. Burt left for White Sulphur Springs and will be joined by Mr. Burt and myself after adjournment.

4 Fort Hill, May 6, 1847

The views you take in reference to Thomas Ritchie...and to the hunker portion of the party are perfectly correct... they are incurably corrupt...and I am glad to be separated from them...to act in accordance to the dictates of my own judgement. Mr. James Polk is the last of the dynasty...the folly and vice of the party have destroyed it...it sought by the Mexican war to perpetuate the power of the party...and will prove the means for his overthrow.

(Polk) will make Zachary Taylor his successor...and that of itself will be sufficient to rally a majority around him. Indeed, it would seem to be an established principle with us, that the party in power, which makes war, will be sure to be turned out of power by it-if successful, by the successful general; and if not, by the opposition. As much as I am opposed to military chieftains for presidents, I shall be content to see him elected against anyone who contributed to the war...I shall stand fast on my own doctrines and act in conformity to them...it is the only way I can serve the country and preserve my own character.

In reference to the letter to you by Mr. Pickens...it is wide of the facts...concerning the falsehoods circulated about me... there is not the slightest foundation that Burt ...expresses anything but friendly feelings...We shall not want to pay off what we owe you, until after the growing crop.

5 Fort Hill, September 8, 1847

I am not all surprised, that you should be discouraged with the results of your planting operations. I still think the place in Edgefield District might be made a valuable one, but it requires skill in management. The land is strong, but a large portion is unkind. It is not a place to be cultivated with success, in the absence of the owner. I feel the extreme wet of the year will greatly injure you, from the want of drains and ditches, and the unabsorbent character of a large portion of the place. I am clearly of the opinion, that, if you are to continue an absentee, you ought to dispose of it, if you can get a fair price, and vest if safely in bonds or stocks, and that you ought to return next year at farthest, in order to determine on your future course.

6 Washington, April 1, 1848

...and that Belgium was so quiet, and disposed to pursue, so wise a course to maintain her institutions and nationality and to prepare to defend them. I hope there will be the same good sense on the part of other European powers. Thus far the revolution in France, exhibits a fair prospect; but I see much to excite in me deep distrust as to the result, indeed. I have no hope that she will ever be able to establish any government deserving to be called a republic. She has on this side of the Atlantick much sympathy but little confidence among the thinking. There is a decided majority in the Senate against hasty action or expression of opinion. The prospect of peace with Mexico still continues good, and the uncertainty, in reference to the Presidential election is still as great as ever.

7 Washington, January 22, 1849

My state of health has been indifferent as of late....Dr. James Hall was called and examined...to the subject of raising the Belgian mission to the grade of a Minister Resident.... My own impression is against the movement as it probably will not succeed and if it did, it would raise up competitors against you.

Quotes from Letters between John C. Calhoun the father, his daughter, and, son

Washington, January 25, 1838

John Calhoun to daughter Anna Clemson

We can not and ought not to live together as we are at present, exposed to the continued attacks and assaults of the other portion of our Union.

Fort Hill, March 18, 1839

John Calhoun to daughter Anna Clemson

The wedding took place at Mr. Armistead Burt's ...a beautiful array of fine looking fashionable girls...supper was tasteful, as you would expect from your cousin Martha Calhoun Burt, who you know has a good deal of ambition and not a small share of taste.

Fort Hill, March 29, 1839

From John Calhoun to son Patrick Calhoun

A good constitution and vigorous health are blessings too high to be sacrificed for any consideration...and it is the greatest folly to suppose, we gain in the end any thing by over working either mind or body.

Fort Hill, January 24, 1841

From Anna Clemson to her father John Calhoun

I have narrowed my correspondence to a very few and I am sure I need not say that if I gave up every one else I would write to you as long as I have strength to hold a pen.

Washington, December 23, 1841

From John Calhoun to daughter Anna Clemson

You are right about the George Washington Statue. Had you been present and examined it minutely your criticism would not have been more correct. Even the colour of the marble from the light, or other cause, looks more like putty than anything else. It is, in my opinion, a failure.

Brussels, April 20, 1846

From Anna Clemson to her father John Calhoun

I am not surprised at this, for you know I have always told you, that the party leaders on either side, were your worst enemies, for a very natural reason. Your disinterested and patriotic course contrasts too strongly with their time serving policy ...know that a wound to our vanity...makes the bitterest enemies.

Fort Hill, August 17, 1847

John Calhoun to daughter Anna Clemson

I am not at all surprised that the victories our arms have achieved in Mexico should make so deep an impression in Europe. We shall, before it terminates (Congressional Session) begin to realize the train of events, to which the Mexican war was destined to lead.

Edgefield District, SC, December 25, 1848

Anna Clemson to her father John Calhoun

Anna quoting a conversation with Col. Pickens, "Oh, Anna, dreadful changes have taken place since you were in Europe...Artful persons have disunited your father and myself"...he was agitated and shed tears and if not sincere, a great actor.

Washington, December 27, 1846
John Calhoun to his daughter Anna Clemson

I desire above all things to save the whole, but if that cannot be, to save the portion where providence has cast my lot, at all events. We never had a darker, or more uncertain future before us.

Brussels, January 22, 1850
Anna Clemson to her father John Calhoun

The long struggle for the Speaker of the US House of Representatives excited much interest in Europe, and some of those who delight in the failure of republics, began already to triumph, and were sadly disappointed.... I may be mistaken... with little confidence one can put in any newspaper statements...I am waiting with impatience for you to tell me what to think.

Brussels, February 18, 1850
Anna Clemson to her father John Calhoun

You can not conceive how miserable I am, at seeing by the last papers that you are ill. And have been ill for ten days. You must quit Washington, my dear father, and resign.

John Calhoun died March 31, 1850.

Brussels, June 24, 1850
Anna Clemson to her brother Patrick Calhoun

Our noble father can never be restored to us. We shall never look upon his like again. In all history I find no man who combined so much talent, heart, philosophy and simplicity. His life proves a firm adherence to principles.

Cherry Hill,
27 July 1839.

My dear Sir;

I will meet you
at the Springs on Tuesday
with great pleasure & will
communicate Martha's message
to her father. As I
do not anticipate any very
great attractions at the Springs
I shall hope to have you here
at an early day.

Very sincerely
yours Geo: McDuffie

Letter from McDuffie to Burt, 1839

Letters from
George McDuffie

Letters from
George McDuffie to Armistead Burt

1 Cherry Hill, November 13, 1833
I have offered to pay the note that you hold for the Estate. I wish you would give it to him and take mine in place...if the money is wanting at any time, I will give a draft on the Charleston Bank.

2 Washington, June 29, 1834
...received a letter from my physician in Philadelphia advising me to proceed immediately to the Virginia Springs... be glad to hear from you frequently during July. In August I may visit the Western States.

3 Cherry Hill, June 6, 1836
It will be out of my power to be present at the dinner for the volunteers...I shall be at home this week and happy to have the company of yourself and Martha.

4 Cherry Hill, March 12, 1837
I want to have been in Washington to attend one of Martha's party...I shall be up some day during Congress...I believe him (a colt) to be the best in the state...

5 Cherry Hill July 19, 1839
...I have learned that you have some idea of going to the Springs shortly and delay your visit to this neighborhood...I now write to request that you will come down immediately.

6 Cherry Hill, July 27, 1839
I will meet you at the Springs on Tuesday with great pleasure and I will communicate Martha's message to her father.

7 Cherry Hill, August 29,1840
...flattered by kind words by my Pendleton friends...I decline the proposed honor... I appreciate the dedication of General Harrison....however. I am a supporter of Mr. Van Buren.

8 Statesburg, SC, November 21, 1847
...but owing to a fall to the floor which deprived me of the use of my leg, I have had a hard time for the last week. Should be very glad if you could come over and see.. Dictated to his daughter.

9 Statesburg, SC, January 18,1848
I have been here nearly two months and have enjoyed a bounty of health. I have had very little of the bad nervous trembling from which I suffer.

Letters from
George McDuffie to John Calhoun

November, 1843
I enclose to you (two letters) from a writer unknown to me, and as he appears to have loose notions of patriotic morality...I would be glad to receive a letter from you at Washington giving your views as to the prospect before us. My fear is that a sufficient number of Van Buren friends will present an adjustment of the tariff.

Pendleton Feby 13th/72

Armistead Burt Esq
   Dear Sir

     Wm Dendy Probate Judge from Walhalla has just delivered to me the letters of administration which I informed you would be given me from his office

     On that score I am happy there will be no further difficulty —

     We are having awful weather, rain, rain, impossible to get out of doors.

     We shall now I hope have the pleasure of receiving that long promised visit

     Mrs Clemsons kind regards

       Very Sincerely
       Thos G. Clemson

Letter from Clemson to Burt, 1872

Letters from
Thomas G. Clemson

Letters from
Thomas Clemson To Armistead Burt

1 Pendleton, February 13, 1872

W.Dendy, *Probate Judge from Walhalla has just delivered to me the letters of administration which I informed you would be given me from his office. On that score I am happy there will be no further difficulty.*

We are having awful weather, rain, rain, impossible to get out of doors. We shall now I hope have the pleasure of receiving that long promised visit. Mrs. Clemson sends her regards.

2 Pendleton, October 17, 1872

Enclosed herewith you will receive a letter from A.O. Norris to Mr. Crayton which explains the difficulty in which we find ourselves. I have no one here that I can call upon except B. Calhoun and his case is such as to preclude the doing so. I therefore send the bond to you signed and suppose that Mr. James Ed. Calhoun would be my surety or perhaps as there is no risk in so small a matter you might perhaps get it arranged in Abbeville.

3 Fort Hill, March 28, 1873

We have a joint and a several interest in the estates of Miss Cornelia Calhoun and under the will of Mrs. Floride Calhoun, to which remoteness of residence and feeble health, render it inconvenience to attend, and we are admonished by declining years that our interests should be ascertained and arranged without further delay. We ask you as our agent and friend to see Mr. Thompson and Mr. Noble with whom our business is to be transacted, and make with them for us the necessary settlement and arrangement concerning our interests and the interests of each of us in the estate of Miss Cornelia Calhoun under the will of her mother Mrs. Floride Calhoun. Your early attention will greatly oblige us.

4 Fort Hill, November 10, 1876

The battle is fought and won. If I would get two wax candles (wax is a liquer) I would burn them one to General Hampton, the other to the Virgin. Judging from the little influence that I had over the blacks, on and about Fort Hill my hopefulness never reached confidence exemplified by the General and yourself. I acknowledge my ignorance. We have workers in this county with some effect it is true, all that I could do on Fort Hill was to gain two who did not vote and I have alone better than many.

5 Fort Hill, January 27, 1877

Not having to state to you that is noteworthy further than to thank you for your political opinions which being hopeful is a good deal in these times of disorder, anarchy, and confusion. Your news corroborates my own, but you are in infinitely better places to form a correct opinion than myself. We are getting to be in as bad a condition as you may have been in Abbeville. And without there be some change of rule we will have to abandon the country. I am too old to live on hope.

6 Fort Hill, June 21, 1878

I have yours of the 21ˢᵗ. Your letter relieved suspense, but I feel worried and merely write to say that your suffering and ill health, gives me much sorrow and pain. Are you sure that the climate (Cashiers Valley) is suited to your condition? Think about it! I have no doubts among your friends in Abbeville that you have attachments and are cared for, but bear in mind, that we are not as young as we have not been, nor what we have been, and age tells.

7 Fort Hill, January 26, 1879

Presume that you have returned from Columbia, I venture to trouble you with a few lines, to hear something about Governor Hampton. So much has been said and so many contradictory accounts are circulated upon all subjects that I am come to believe that we are in a metaphorical age, from which may we be delivered. But that even will surely not come in my lifetime, it may in yours, for you are exceptional like Methuselah. May it be so! I wrote you some time back that I had offered Fort Hill to parties for sale. I hope it is under consideration by those who applied, I having made answer in the affirmative, but I doubt much considering the impecunious condition of all parties, save lawyers, from what would have been the richest state in the Union.

8 Fort Hill, December 1879-January 1780

General Hampton, with whom I had a few moments conversation when in Columbia last week, told me that he had received a letter from you, in which you had stated that you were still sick. Yours of the 11th dated Cashiers Valley informed me that you are better and that you leave for Abbeville on the next day the 12th. I sincerely hope that your better continues and you are by this time in your usual health. General Hampton looked very well and walked without a crutch, which I was very pleased to remark. We have unfavorable news from the Indiana and Ohio. The anxious suspense will soon be over, when I hope we shall be at rest and free from the metaphorical sayings of demagogues and lying politicians.

9 Fort Hill, August 30, 1980

Since my writing you as I promised to do on my arrival here, we have had a continuation of intense sun light, which my short visit to the mountains rendered my eyes (better). Since I am back I am forced to keep the blinds closed until the night when I do not suffer. On my short visit to the mountains, I have learned that Oconee Station is the best and shortest route to Cashiers Valley.

Letters from
Thomas G. Clemson To John C. Calhoun

1 Brussels Belgium, June 27, 1846

It did not surprise me to hear of the severe rains that had fallen in the South West, for nature is full of compensations, and during the last year Europe has been very wet whilst in the United States, there had been little rain...The sandy soil on which this city is built makes rain essential to vegetation and comfort of the inhabitants...when ever it is dry the air becomes filled with a fine dust which penetrates every where...I perceive he House of Representatives has had under consideration the Diplomatic bill...The consular system is rotten, and something should be done. I am the only Unites States functionary that has been in Belgium since last December... So far as our diplomatic functionaries are concerned, you are doubtless aware of the necessity of reform...including the emoluments according to position...increased pay to resident ministers...permanent carriages...complete sense of respectability at all times. I know you must see and deplore many things that are out of your power to remedy...the war with Mexico has its good and bad effects. Everything that can be turned against us by the public prints is made use of to throw the US....into false and disgraceful position....everything that can be said against us is eagerly caught and magnified...If we could now bring about an honourable peace and retire from the Mexican territory without the usual excess that invariably follow successful armies, it would be a great point gained.

2 Blankenberghe, Belgium, August 11, 1846

I read your report (on the Memphis Convention) and its premises appear to be conclusive...and produced the effect of uniting the West and South... to break up old party lines and bring about a new order of things. The whole subject now requires popular and wide spread discussion. The Washington Union as a paper can not have much force among thinking men, but there is weight in the position it holds ...which are made use of to act on the masses which is all they require...There appears to be a great want of thinking papers in the United States.

3 Brussels Belgium, March 28,1847

The delivery of a file of Thomas Richie's scurrilous paper the Washington Union *in which you are not spared...damning you with insidious remarks in his own peculiar style. ...I agree with you that this war has been disastrous and might have been avoided. It is the height of folly to suppose that we can carry our arms easily to Mexico. The file contained a letter from Col. Francis Pickens...refuting falsehoods about his splitting with Mr. Calhoun...only regretting that Calhoun had not supported the supplies for the Mexican war...including a quote " Mr. Calhoun's friends (who by the by are no real friends of his in this State) have injured him very much. They have advised for their selfish purposes and not for his interests." In speaking of cotton Mr. Pickens thinks that the defect in last years cotton crop below the falls of the rivers of the Gulf of Mexico by the worm and mist is thought to be a permanently uncertain production of that region. I see no prospect of a relative increase income in my moneyed income from planting. I do not know your intentions are on the debt that is owed me...it should be expressed in a more permanent shape...I have felt gratified that my salary sufficed (or nearly so) the wants of myself and family... for the last six months I have been diligently employed in perfecting myself in studies that will always be a resource at least of pleasure.*

backgammon & fish in full

As the news from Washington
seems to indicate an early
adjournment. I hope that it
will not be necessary for me
to return there. & I shall try to
set off to Va in a short time.
Do let me hear from you
Did you receive my letter from
Washn? Hoping to see you soon
I am
very truly Yrs
Wade Hampton

Hon. A. Burt—

Letter from Hampton to Burt

Letters from
Wade Hampton III

Letters from
Wade Hampton to Armistead Burt
1868-1881

1 Wildwoods Plantation, MS March 13, 1868

My business has given me such trouble that I have been compelled to remain here on a small scale to look after it. Unfortunately with the results of this year's planting, I desire to consult you to give me the benefit of your advice.... My creditors have brought suit against me for bankruptcy. No other choice. My land is all that I have. I cannot pay my debts. Give me our opinion. You are the only one I have consulted.

2 Wildwoods Plantation, MS, Early in 1869

I am now bankrupt, no choice to me. The land is valueless. On Christmas Eve, December 24, 1868, Hampton filed a petition for bankruptcy protection in the courts in Jackson, MS with a total debt of $1,012,328. (In 1861, Wade Hampton had owned 12,000 acres of productive land.)

3 Columbia, SC, July 4, 1869

...Hope you are able to accompany us to the mountains. (Cashiers Valley). I have requested that Christopher find you a house and Edward could furnish it for you. You will not need to take anything but sheets and pillowcases and yourself.

4 Fairfield, SC, September 8, 1870

I have written to Mr. Parker sending the letter to your care, asking him to let McDuffie come up on Friday the 16th. Will you do me the favor to look after him as he is ailing? I have written to Colonel Beaseley to send the information. I am requesting your opinion on the publication I have sent.

5 Wild Woods, SC, 1871

I have great pleasure in complying with your request. Indeed I have wanted for sometime to consult you as to the condition of affairs in our unhappy state. What has been done since the defeat of the Reform Party? What are we to do? The objects of our Reform friends were praise worthy but their whole plan of battle was wrong. They fought notably and deserve well of all our people and have not one word of blame to say of them but can we not profit by their misfortune and their experience as to win the next fight. Present indications are for the benefit of the Democratic Party in the next formal election. I still entertain the opinion once expressed to you that the only salvation for the people lies in the triumph of that party. We may not be able to carry the state in the Presidential election, but if we can secure a majority or even a strong minority in our legislature, we will be on the way to permanent relief. This way the plan and all the details we can consult about and digest to determine if still regarded as favorable. It may be that we can carry the state. If we in the Presidential election promise to be done, they may be willing to struggle for the vote of our state. It seems to me our first step should be to set the election date of the state changed. The people and the Grand Juries should demand this change so as to ensure a fair expression of popular opinion. In a fair election I think that we might carry the state but we can never under the present conditions. Our members of the legislature can accomplish much if they are active and determined and should be strongly backed up. Can they not get the removal of all our disabilities of the people? You are on the spot and can see more clearly than myself. What is about to be done and what can be done? I will do all I can and to aid any effect to relieve our people and I beg you to consult fully to me on matters political. We are getting on here in the same slipboard that has existed for the last few years. The crops were very fine but much of the cotton is wanting because the workers refuse to pick it. The climate is very disheartening and until we can put other crops in the place I see no help for us. I shall rent all the land I can this year, so that the Negroes may want their own cotton.

6 Columbia, SC September 1, 1871 & September 15, 1871

Mary thinks that you have a chair that her father, George McDuffie used while he was ill. If so, she begs you let her have it. I know it will give you pleasure to send it to her.

The chair has arrived safely and Mary is much obliged to you for sending it.

7 Baltimore, MD, December 28, 1872 Baltimore Fire Extinguisher Works, Hampton as President

I am much gratified of your estimate. Your opinion as a critic of this enterprise stands very high with me. The copy of the publication you had sent me was so badly printed that I could use another. I feel that all villages and county business will adopt this machinery. Perhaps Abbeville will get one of the equipment and I will that you would bring the matter to the attention of the authority.

Hampton elected Governor by Democratic Party
8 Columbia, SC November 19, 1876'

We have now a great victory, but we still have to face heavy responsibilities and arduous duties.

9 Columbia, SC, March 24, 1878

Your letter reached me and I should be very pleased to accept the invitation as always, but I fear my doing so would put McGowan to inconvenience. Do say to him that his place to meet me is in Anderson. I have no idea that there were to be any political meetings and I do not intend to make there the opening of a campaign.... there would be a manifest impropriety in my taking any such action before his meeting of the convention. I will consult with you fully when we meet. The opposition has been crushed out.

10 Columbia, SC, May 17, 1881

What are your plans for the summer? As the Valley does not seem to agree with you why not the Virginia Springs. I am sure that your health will be improved. I think that I shall spend sometime there. I sent you a circular about Daggar Springs. All of the springs in Virginia would be helpful for all people with rheumatism.

11 Dagger Springs, VA, August 28, 1881

I hope you will soon again have your strength and be able to visit here before October and then go to the Springs with us. The White Sulphur Springs has too many celebrities and has been too crowded for comfort. I have been suffering from my leg and several pieces of bone have come out.

Sources and Citations

Specific Citations are listed by Source with the page number (p.0) of the use of the reference.

Manuscripts and Letters

Burts, Jr. Robert M, "The Life of Armistead Burt" (Master of Arts thesis, 1945) Duke University Library.
  Citation #9 (p.8)
  Citation #31 Personal Interview, Mrs. William Greene, 1942 (p.17)

Burt, Armistead, Letters and Papers. Duke University Library.
  Citation #6 1845 (p.7)
  Citation #11 January 1, 1845 (p.9)
  Citation# 19. Edward Noble to Burt, 1862 (p.12)
  Citation #23 A.J. Simond to Burt April 3, 1868 (p.14)

Calhoun, John C. Letters, Private and Political, 1765-1850. Duke University Library.
  Citation #1 December 27, 1831 (p.5)
  Citation #2 January 15, 1833 (p.6)

Clemson, Thomas Greene, Papers. Special Collections Unit. Clemson University Library.

Davis, Jefferson, Manuscripts. Duke University Library.
  Citation #18 April 26, 1861 (p.12)

Hampton, Wade III, Manuscripts,1799-1890. Duke University Library.
  Citation #26 (p.16)

Perry, Benjamin F. ,Papers 1822-1933."Scrapbook I," University of North Carolina Library.
  Citation #3 (p.6)

Pickens, Francis W., Manuscripts. Duke University Library.
  Citation #17 January 31, 1861 (p.12)

Special Collections Unit, South Caroliniana Library, University of South Carolina.

Books

Andrew, Rod, Jr., *Confederate Warrior to Southern Redeemer*, Chapel Hill: University of North Carolina Press, 2008.

Bennett, Alma, editor, *Thomas Greene Clemson*, Clemson: Clemson University Digital Press, 2009.

Cooper, Jr. William J., *Jefferson Davis' America*, NY: Vintage Civil War Library, Vintage Books, 2000.

Edmonds, Bobby F. *George McDuffie: Southern Orator*, McCormick County: Cedar Hill, 2007.

Edmonds, Bobby F., *Land of Cotton, Published Speeches of George McDuffie*, McCormick County: Cedar Hill, 2011.
    Citation #36 (p.54)

Helsley, Alexia Jones, *Hidden History of Greenville County*, Charleston: The History Press, 2009.

Henning, Helen Kohn, *Great South Carolinians of a Later Date, Volume II*, Chapel Hill: University of North Carolina Press, 1949.

Magoon, E. L., *Living Orators of America*, NY, 1850.
    Citation #37 (p.55)

MacLeod, James L, *The Great Doctor Waddel*, Greenville, NC: Southern Historical Press, 1985.
    Citation #39 (p.85)

Periodicals

Abbeville Press and Banner. Abbeville, SC.
    Citation #5 April 15, 1846 (p.7)
    Citation #14 April 10 1856 (p.10)
    Citation #15 June 28, 1861 (p.10)
    Citation #16 November 23, 1860 (p.10)
    Citation #20 October 31, 1883 (p.12)

Citation #24 April 2, 1869 (p.15)
Citation #25 October 5, 1865 (p.15)
Citation #29 November 23, 1883 (p.16)
Citation #30 November 23, 1883 (p.17)
Citation #32 November 21,1883 (p.18)
Citation #34 June 1861(p.23)

Congressional Globe. Appendix 2 Sess.p570. US Congress.
    Citation #7 (p.7)

Edgefield Advertizer. Edgefield, SC.
    Citation #4 September 14, 1842 (p.6)
    Citation #8 June 19, 1852 (p.8)
    Citation #10 July 12 1852 (p.14)
    Citation #12 February 26, 1852 (p.9)
    Citation #13 March 9, 1853 (p.9)
    Citation #33 March 9, 1853 (p.21)

Pamphlets, Papers, and Websites

Clemson.edu, Clemson University.
    Citation #39 "Clemson Story" (p. 67)
    Citation #40 "Historic Properties" (p.66)

"Confederate Catechism of Secession in Abbeville County 1860-1865," Confederate States Pamphlets 1, No VI, p 6.
    Citation #22 (p.13)

"Proceedings of the Taxpayers Convention of South Carolina," Columbia. February 17- 20, 1874, p.6.
    Citation #27 (p.16)

"South Carolina Reports, I-XV, 1868-1882," Columbia, 1868.
    Citation #28 March 13, 1868 (p.16)

Waters, Marshall P. III, PhD. "The Missing Confederate Gold," *Surratt Courier Newsletter,* December 2009. Maryland. Surratt Society & The Maryland-National Capital Park Commission.
    Citation #21 (p.23)
    Citation #36 (p.37)

S. Robert Lathan, Jr. M.D., the author, in his personal library

Bob Lathan, author of *Who Was Armistead Burt*," spent almost ten years searching for information to accurately describe the life and connections of Armistead Burt. A rewarding research trip took him to the area of the old Abbeville District that was home to Burt and most of the people of the Southern Leadership Network. The author's visit with Mrs. Hutchinson and Mr. Edmonds pointed him the direction of the landmarks that reference original homesites. Additional investigations provided interesting books, manuscripts, and letters, a few of which are now included in Bob's own library.